FOLLOWING
JESUS

FOLLOWING JESUS

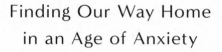

Finding Our Way Home
in an Age of Anxiety

HENRI J. M. NOUWEN

EDITED BY
GABRIELLE EARNSHAW

CONVERGENT

NEW YORK

Copyright © 2019 by The Henri Nouwen Legacy Trust

All rights reserved.
Published in the United States by Convergent Books, an imprint of
Random House, a division of Penguin Random House LLC, New York.
crownpublishing.com

CONVERGENT BOOKS is a registered trademark and its C colophon
is a trademark of Penguin Random House LLC.

For more information about Henri Nouwen, his work, and the work of
the Henri Nouwen Society, visit www.HenriNouwen.org.

Published in association with Alive Literary Agency, 7680 Goddard
Street, Suite 200, Colorado Springs, Colorado 80920,
www.aliveliterary.com

Library of Congress Cataloging-in-Publication Data is available upon
request.

ISBN 978-1-101-90639-2
Ebook ISBN 978-1-101-90640-8

Printed in Canada

Book design by Songhee Kim

10 9 8 7 6 5 4 3 2 1

First Edition

CONTENTS

FOREWORD

Henri Nouwen: My Friend and Teacher

I first heard of Henri Nouwen while still in seminary in Ohio in the late 1960s. My mother wrote me from Kansas that there was a new Dutch priest serving at our parish, and she loved to attend his Masses. "His accent makes him hard to understand, but he says the Mass with such reverence and devotion," she told me. Of course, at the time, I had no idea who she was talking about. He was then a doctoral student of psychology at the Menninger institute, near our family home in Topeka. But it was not long before he entered my life.

Starting in the mid-1970s, we were often speakers at the same conferences. Soon he visited me several times at the New Jerusalem Community in Cincinnati, where he told me how he longed for community and intimate relationships. I could tell it was a passionate need. We would go for walks from time to time in the working-class neighborhood where the community had settled. He would invariably entertain me (I do not know what other word to use) with his endless spiritual curiosity, his extreme vulnerability, and his humble concern for people.

Henri longed for in-depth relationship, and I think relationship was, in fact, his real genius. He could spot the authentic from the inauthentic, and longed to be a healer of the inauthentic. Which is exactly how he served us all so well!

When I moved to New Mexico in 1986 to found the Center for Action and Contemplation, Henri wrote me a very supportive letter encouraging me to "teach nothing but contemplation"! And he even recommended to my study the writings of Eknath Easwaran. This showed me the depth of his Christian faith that was not threatened by a Hindu-based teacher from India. It also showed me that as Catholic as he was, he recognized authentic contemplative teaching wherever it came from.

Because I looked up to him as a wise and holy elder, I would often try to get some free spiritual direction out of him. Only a few minutes into it, I'd realize that he never really answered my questions, but had somehow turned it around to make me into his spiritual director! I was never sure if it was humility on his part or some kind of unconscious need for reciprocity, but I finally concluded that it was a totally sincere spiritual search and he valued my insights as much as his own. As much as I knew that he was a spiritual writer, in real life he was a spiritual seeker and believer—always filled with desire for more wisdom and for more capacity to love.

When he heard that I was beginning to teach a spirituality for men, he wrote me and strongly encouraged me in this regard. He also told a number of artists that they needed to paint images that could be healing for the so often broken father-son relationship. He knew that it often took visual images to begin the healing process. At least one iconographer, the Franciscan Robert Lentz, took his advice and painted John the Beloved with his head on the breast of Jesus. Henri loved it, and was very honest with me and others about his complex relationship with his own father.

All in all, and from my simple perspective, these were Henri Nouwen's primary gifts: *human vulnerability and the healing power that he gained from such rugged honesty.* For most of us, he created the very phrase "the wounded healer" and fully exemplified it in his life. He loved being well known and yet fully saw the irony. I remember when he said to me with sincere hurt, "My own family in the Netherlands does not read my books, or even know about them!" But then he would also laugh at himself for saying such a thing.

Maybe we could say that Henri invited the human shadow into the entire conversation of spirituality, similar to Francis of Assisi and Thérèse of Lisieux, but with more psychological savvy. This led him to so much practical insight into the nature of love and all relationship, especially God's love. We Christians had grown used to calling the shadow self "sin" and perhaps quickly confessing it as such, but then were incapable of learning from it. Henri surely "confessed" his sins and failures to those close to him—but only after he had first felt their sting, their texture, their truth, and their always available wisdom. These honest acknowledgments seemed to lead him to compassion for others.

With all of this, and because of all of this, Henri emerged as a superb Christian teacher who will surely stand the test of time. And you are now about to enjoy some of his hard-won wisdom in this book.

He will soon be your friend, if he is not already.

Fr. Richard Rohr, O.F.M.

Center for Action and Contemplation

Albuquerque, New Mexico

INTRODUCTION

Are you following Jesus? I want you to look at yourself and ask that question.

Are you a follower? Am I?

Often, we are more wanderers than followers. I am speaking of myself as much as of you. We are people who run around a lot, do many things, meet many people, attend many events, read many books. We are very involved. We experience life as many, many things. We go here, we go there, we do this, we do that, we speak to him, we speak to her, we have this to do and that to do. Sometimes we wonder how we can do it all. If we sit down and think about it, we are often running from one emergency to another. We are so busy and so involved. Yet if we are asked what we are so busy with we don't really know.

People who wander from one thing to the other, feeling that they are lived more than they live, are very tired. Deeply tired. It is a problem for many people.

It is not so much that we do many things but rather that we do many things while wondering whether anything is happening. Sometimes it seems as though we have all these balls up in the air and wonder how we can keep them all going. It is very tiring. Exhausting actually.

Some people finally stop and give it all up. They say, "It was five years and nothing happened anyway." They sit there and do nothing. Nothing excites them anymore. They have no real interest in life. They just watch television, read comic books, and sleep all the time. There is no rhythm, no movement, no tension. Sometimes there is escape through alcohol, drugs, or sex, but nothing fascinates them. Nothing energizes them.

"What do you want to do?" "I don't care."

"Want to go to a movie?" "I don't care."

They have moved from wandering to just sitting there. These people are also very tired. There is a real fatigue there. Both types of people, the running-around ones and the just-sitting-there ones, are not moving anywhere.

There is something of the wanderer and something of the person who just sits there in all of us. If you look at this world you might think, "I am so tired. There is so much fatigue, so much experience of heaviness in this world, that I find myself sometimes as a wanderer and sometimes as a sitter." It is into this deeply tired world of ours that God sends Jesus to speak the voice of love. Jesus says, "Follow me. Don't keep running around. Follow me. Don't just sit there. Follow me."

The voice of love is the voice that can completely reshape our life from a wandering or just-sitting-there life to one that is focused and has a point to go to.

"Follow me."

Some of us may have heard this voice already. Others not.

Once we hear the voice calling us to follow, things often fall into place. Instead of moving in many different directions, suddenly we have focus. We know where we are going. We have only one concern. Suddenly, that deep boredom we experienced vanishes because we have heard the voice of love.

If we don't have a focus, if we don't have anyone to follow, we are empty people. We are! Yet, when we discover that there is a voice of love calling us and saying, "Follow me," everything becomes different. The life that seemed so dull, so boring, so exhausting suddenly is a life that has a direction.

We might say to ourselves, "Now I know why I am living!"

This book has been written to help you and me to hear that voice of love, to hear that voice that whispers in your ear, "Follow me."

What I hope to do is guide us from restless wandering to joyful following; from being bored people just sitting there doing nothing to being excited because we have heard a voice.

The voice is not a voice that will force itself on us. It is a voice of love, and love doesn't push or pull. Love is very sensitive.

There is a beautiful story in the Old Testament where the prophet stands at the mouth of a cave and the Lord is passing. There is thunder, and the Lord is not in the thunder. There is an earthquake, and the Lord is not in the earthquake. There is fire, and the Lord is not in the fire. Then there is a still, small voice, and the Lord is in that voice. (See 1 Kings 19:11–13.)

The voice is very sensitive. It can be very quiet. It is sometimes hard to hear. But the voice of love is already in you. You may have already heard it.

Start trying to hear that voice. Get quiet and spend some time trying to hear it.

Listen. It says, "I love you," and calls you by name. It says, "Come, come. Follow me."

Dear Lord,

Be with me today. Listen to my confusion and help me know how to live it. I don't know the words. I don't know the way. Show me the way. You are a quiet God. Help me to listen to your voice in a noisy world. I want to be with you. I know you are peace. I know you are joy. Help me to be a peaceful and joyful person. These are the fruits of living close to you. Bring me close to you, dear Lord.

AMEN

＊

CHAPTER ONE

THE INVITATION
"Come and See"

As John the Baptist stood there with two of his disciples, Jesus passed and John stared hard at him and said: "Look, there is the Lamb of God." Hearing this, the two disciples followed Jesus, and Jesus turned around, saw them following, and said, "What do you want?" "Rabbi [which means "teacher"], where do you live?" "Come and see," he replied. So they went and saw where he lived and they stayed with him the rest of the day. It was about the tenth hour.

JOHN 1:35–39

Imagine you are in this story for a moment. Imagine you are there with John the Baptist. He was a tough man. Picture him dressed in camel hair. He is separate from others. With a stern voice he says, "Repent! Repent! You are sinful people. Repent, repent, repent!"

People are there listening. Somehow they feel that there is something missing in their lives. Somehow they feel that they are busy with many things and exhausted or they are just sitting there and nothing is ever going to happen.

They go to this strange man—this wild man—and listen. John and Andrew, two of John's disciples, are there with him. One day Jesus passes by. John looks hard at him and says, "That is the Lamb of God who takes away the sins of the world."

John knew that his people were sinners and needed to repent, but he also knew that he could not take away the sins of those people; that taking away sins was not a human possibility. He said, "Repent, repent, repent!" But when Jesus passed by, John looked hard at him, and said to John and Andrew, "Look, *that* is the Lamb of God that takes away the sins of the world. That is the servant of God. He came to suffer. That is the One who has been sent to become the sacrifice, the Lamb of God, so that he can take away your sins."

Just be there in this picture.

Just be there where John and Andrew are, eager to start a new life, with a new focus, a new beginning, a new heart, a new soul. Those two young men start following Jesus, and Jesus turns around and sees them following him and said, "What do you want?" And what do they say? Do they say, "Lord, we want to be your followers," "Lord, we want to do your will," "Lord, we want you to take our sins away"? They don't say any of that! Instead, they ask, "Where do you live?"

Somehow, right here in the beginning of the story we hear a very important question: Where do you live? What is your place? What is your way? How is it to be around you?

Jesus says, "Come and see."

He doesn't say, "Come into my world." He doesn't say, "Come, I will change you." He doesn't say, "Become my disciples," "Listen to me," "Do what I tell you," "Take up your cross." No. He says, "Come and see. Look around. Get to know me." That is the invitation.

They stayed with him. They went and saw where he lived and stayed with him the rest of the day. John says it was about the tenth hour, or four o'clock in the afternoon.

Jesus invited them and they came around him and they dwelled with him. They went willingly to his place. They saw a man very different from John the Baptist, who yelled, "Repent, repent, repent! The time has come." Instead, Jesus said, "Come see where I live."

They saw Jesus, the Lamb of God. The humble servant. Poor, gentle, warm, peacemaker, pure of heart. They saw him. Already then. They saw the Lamb of God.

There is a softness. There is a gentleness. There is a humility.

"Come and see."

"They stayed with him for the rest of the day."

Jesus invites them in to just look around.

Be there. Look with the eyes of the heart to the story you have heard.

We Are Invited

Jesus is offering an invitation to come into the House of God. It is an invitation to enter into God's dwelling place.

It is not an invitation with harsh demands. It is the story of the Lamb of God saying to us, "Come. Come to my home. Look around. Don't be afraid." Long before Jesus' radical call to leave everything behind, Jesus says, "Come, have a look where I am."

Jesus is a host who wants us around him. Jesus is the Good Shepherd of the Old Testament who invites his people to his table where the cup of life overflows.

This image of God inviting us to his home is used throughout scripture.

The Lord is my house. The Lord is my hiding place. The Lord is my awning.

The Lord is my refuge. The Lord is my tent. The Lord is my temple. The Lord is my dwelling place. The Lord is my home. The Lord is the place where I want to dwell all the days of my life.

God wants to be our room, our house. He wants to be anything that makes us feel at home. She is like a bird hugging us under her wings. She is like a woman holding us in her womb. She is Infinite Mother, Loving Host, Caring Father, the Good Provider who invites us to join him.

There is a sense of being that is safe, that is good. In this dangerous world full of violence, chaos, and destruction, there is this place where we want to be. We want to be in the House of God—to feel safe, to be embraced, to be loved, to be cared for. With the psalmist we say, "Where else does my heart want to stay but in the House of the Lord?" (See Psalms 84 and 27.)

The word "home" continues to grow in significance. Jesus says, "I am going to the house of my Father to prepare a room for you because in the house of my Father there are many dwelling places" (John 14:2). Jesus tells us about that great home, that mansion, where we will have a banquet and the cup is overflowing, where life will be one great celebration.

John's Gospel opens with an incredible vision of home. "In the beginning was the Word, and the Word was with God, and the Word was God, and in the Word everything was created, and the Word became flesh and pitched its tent among us" (John 1:1–3, 14). Home is what the incarnation is all about. If you read the Gospel you hear how Jesus speaks: "I have made my home in you so you can make your home in me"

(John 15:4–8). This vision of the House of God goes deeper and deeper. Suddenly, all these images merge and we realize that we are God's home and that we are invited to make our home where God has made God's home. We realize that right where we are, right here in this body, with this face, with these hands, with this heart, we are the place where God can dwell.

Listen carefully: Jesus wants you and me to become part of the intimate family of God. "Just as the Father loves me so I love you" (John 15:9). Jesus says, "You are no longer slaves, strangers and outsiders; no, you are friends because everything I have heard from my Father is yours, all the works I do you can do, and even greater ones. I am not the great person and you the little one—no, all that I can do, you can do too" (John 15:15–16).

The intimate relationship between the Father and the Son has a name. It is Spirit. Holy Spirit. "I want you to have my Spirit." "Spirit" means "breath." It comes from the ancient Greek word *pneuma*. "I want you to have my breathing. I want you to have that most intimate part of me so that the relationship that is between you and God is the same as between me and God, which is a divine relationship."

What you need to hear with your heart is that you are invited to dwell in the family of God. You are invited to be part of that intimate communion right now.

The spiritual life means you are part of the family of God.

When we say "I say this in the name of Jesus" or "I do this in the name of Jesus," we really mean "I do it from the place of God." A lot of people today think that if we do something in the name of Jesus it is because Jesus is not there so we do it as a representative of his. But that is not what it means. To speak in the name of Jesus, to dwell in the name of Jesus, to act in the name of Jesus, means that the name is where I am. Where are you? "I am alive in the name and that is where I dwell, that is where my home is." Once you are living there, you can go out into the world without ever leaving that place.

Outside of that place, outside of the heart of Jesus, all of our words and all of our thoughts add up to nothing. Whatever you do, never leave that place, because only in that place are you in God. Only from that place comes salvation, and salvation is what we have to bring forth into this world.

The invitation is "Come and see the place of God." In the beginning we think it is just his home, his physical place, but as the Gospel of John develops, John shows us that the place of God is the intimate life of God himself—the Father, Son, and Spirit who form a family of love into which we are invited. Following Jesus is the way to enter into that family of love.

We do not have to follow Jesus. First is the invitation. "Come, come. Come and see."

How Do We Respond?

Listen

You respond to the invitation by listening to people like John the Baptist. If John hadn't said, "Look! There is the Lamb of God," John and Andrew might have missed him. The Gospel story shows that we have to listen to somebody else who points us to Jesus. We don't find Jesus on our own.

This person may not be exciting, attractive, or easy. The person who points to Jesus might bug the heck out of us precisely because of our prejudices. We may disregard this person and say, "Look how he dresses." "I don't care for the kind of people who talk about Jesus."

I want you to realize that we need to listen to these people even if they are not necessarily the ones we feel so comfortable with. Maybe they are too poor. Or they are too rich. Or they have a strange accent. Or they speak in a different language. Somehow there is always a reason to say, "Well, they themselves have got problems."

And yet. They point to Jesus.

We need to listen to people who are not necessarily easy to listen to. It might be a very simple woman, a very simple man, who says, "Do you love Jesus?" And you say, "Oh, come on."

Listen.

Be aware.

It might be a very powerful man, maybe the Pope himself, who speaks of Jesus, and you might say, "Well, it's easy if you live in the Vatican with all that stuff around you." But it doesn't matter. Listen.

It might be a very untraditional person who doesn't follow all the rules. But when someone calls you to "follow Jesus," be careful. Take that voice very seriously.

"Look! Look, the Lamb of God!"

We can come up with a thousand arguments not to look, not to listen. But be very careful.

Listen.

If you do not, you might never find Jesus. Those who point to Jesus point away from themselves to him. Take that seriously.

The Old Testament tells us that Samuel was sleeping in the temple and the Lord says, "Samuel, Samuel!" He then goes to Eli, the priest, and says, "I keep hearing this voice." At first Eli says, "Go back to bed." Finally Eli realizes that God was calling the boy and says, "God is speaking to you." Later, when Samuel hears the voice again, he responds, "Here I am, Lord, your servant is listening" (1 Samuel 3:1–9). Without Eli, Samuel would not have known that God was speaking to him. Without John the Baptist, John and Andrew would not have looked at Jesus. We have to listen to the people in our lives, even the broken ones, and take them very seriously.

Ask

After listening, we have to ask.

John and Andrew ask, "Where do you live?" It is very important that we want to know who Jesus is if we want to follow him. That we *really* want to know.

"Lord, where do you live? We want to be with you. We want some idea of what you are about."

You have to ask. I have to ask.

Keep asking.

"Lord, how is it to be with you? I want to follow you but I am not so sure."

Keep asking.

"I have seen people doing things I don't really like. Show me what you are like so I can see for myself. Show me. Where do you live?"

This is where our prayers start. Our prayers start when we say, "Lord, give me a sense of who you are. Some people say this about you, other people say that about you, but I want a real sense of who you are for myself."

Do not be afraid to ask.

Jesus says, "I no longer call you servants anymore. I call you friends because I tell you everything" (John 15:15). We have to pray for that interest. Pray, "Lord, I just want to know you. Give me a sense of who you are so I can speak out of that experience." Think of John the Evangelist, who says, "What we have seen with our own eyes, heard with our own ears, touched with our own hands" (1 John 1:1). That is what I want for us. To want to talk about what we have seen, what we have heard.

Dwell

The third response to the invitation is to dwell. "John and Andrew stayed the whole afternoon until four o'clock." We have to dwell with Jesus. We have to dare to just be there with him. Be very quiet, be very still. Just dwell there. In John's Gospel Jesus says, "I want to dwell with you. I want to be your friend. You are not a servant. You are part of my household. Visit me. Stay here. Spend time with me. Dwell with me."

To follow Jesus you have to be willing to say, "This half hour I am going to dwell with Jesus. I know I will be distracted. I know I will have a hundred thoughts and a million things to do. But I know you love me and invite me, even when I am antsy and anxious. I am going to dwell."

Be with him and listen. Listen to the One who invites you. Be quiet. Like a child dwells in the house with her mother and father. Just dwell. Play around. Be there. A half hour a day. Is it possible? Is it possible for half an hour? Just be there. Sit there and do nothing. Waste time with Jesus. That is what love does. Love always wants to be with her lover. You want to be there. Enjoy it. "It is so good to be here with you, Jesus" (Mark 9:5).

Slowly, we discover that we are building a home in

the Lord and that we are in His house not just for the half hour but for the whole day. We are always in the House of the Lord. We are in a place of the Lord wherever we are, whatever we do. We are already home.

Even when we are on the way to our house we are home.

Don't say, "I am too busy." Don't say, "I have better things to do." Just be there. Every day. Pray and discover. We can live in this hostile, competitive world and be at home.

Listen, ask, and dwell, and you will slowly grow in Jesus.

FOLLOWING JESUS IS different from following a famous person or joining a movement.

What do I mean by this?

A lot of people are "pulled in," "seduced by," or "drawn into" things or people. Hero worship is exactly that. We are pulled in by singers and movie stars. These people have the power to seduce us into another world and we are, in a certain sense, passively drawn into them. This is not following. People might think it is following—like following a folk hero—but this is not the following that Jesus speaks about.

We are also not followers by being attracted to movements, even good ones. People often ask me, "What are you into these days? Are you into co-counseling, primal scream, psychosynthesis, ESP, intellectual analysis? What are you into?" We learn from these movements and are attracted to them, but what the Gospel speaks about is something else altogether. The spiritual journey is essentially different from being "pulled into" a hero worship situation or being attracted to a very good movement.

There are all kinds of interesting movements: healing movements, therapeutic movements, and so forth. I myself have been part of many of them. But what is typical of these other forms of following is that they are usually centered on "me." If you are pulled into hero worship you will find yourself looking for a vicarious self. I spoke with friends who went to a Beatles concert years ago and heard how easy it was to lose their identity to those boys from Liverpool. My friends were swept up. They weren't here anymore. They were vicariously there. In a way they merged themselves with the music and those people. In joining these movements we are usually searching for some inner harmony, for some healing solution to some pain. We hope that maybe this movement or that will give us more emotional balance or a new inner unity.

Yet when Jesus says, "Follow me," something very different is happening. We enter into a different way of following because it is a call away from "me" and toward God. It is a call to let God enter into the center of our being. It is a willingness to let go of "me," of "I," and to gradually say, "You, Lord, are the One."

It is not a way of searching for the self, but a way of emptying, of leaving the self to create space for a whole new way of being that is of God. Jesus' life was an increasing giving up of himself so that God could be totally at the center. This is what the crucifixion is all about. When Jesus says, "Follow me," he is saying, "Leave that place of the self. Leave mother, father, brother, sister, home, familiar possessions. Leave your 'me' world—my mother, my brother, my sister, my possessions, my world—and follow me."

Jesus says, "Leave it." Leave it so that God can enter into the center.

We are invited to leave the familiar place and find God. We are invited to find God and trust that in God we'll discover who we truly are. The emphasis is not "me" but the Lord.

Following Jesus is focusing on the One who calls and gradually trusting that we can let go of our familiar world and that something new will come.

We will become new people!

We will get a new name!

Abram answered God's call and he became Abraham. Saul followed Jesus, he became Paul. Simon followed Jesus and became Peter. Peter left his own, old world and entered into God's world and found who he truly was in God.

What is your new name? What is mine?

Lord Jesus,

Help me in this moment to set aside all that
has preoccupied me today.

Take away the many fears that rage around
me. Take away the many feelings of insecurity
and low self-esteem, and let me be shaped by
you, the Lamb of God.

Help me to enter more deeply into your
silence, where I can listen to you and hear
how you call me, and find the strength and
courage to follow you. I ask you to be with me
as I listen to your word and come to a deeper
understanding of your mystery of calling me
to follow you.

Be with me now and always.

AMEN

CHAPTER TWO

THE CALL
"Come Follow Me"

Here is a story of how Jesus called the first disciples:

Once while Jesus was standing beside the lake of Gennesaret, the sea of Galilee, and the crowd was pressing in on him to hear the word of God, he saw two boats there at the shore of the lake; the fishermen had gone out of them and were washing their nets. He got into one of the boats, the one belonging to Simon, and asked him to put out a little way from the shore. Then he sat down and taught the crowds from the boat. When he had finished speaking, he said to Simon, "Put out into the deep water and let down your nets for a catch." Simon answered, "Master, we have worked all night long but have caught nothing. Yet if you say so, I will let down the nets." When they had done this, they caught so many fish that their nets were beginning to break. So they signaled their partners in the other boat to come and help them. And they came and filled both boats, so that they began to sink. But when Simon Peter saw it, he fell down at Jesus' knees, saying, "Go away from me, Lord, for I am a sinful man!" For he and all who were with him were amazed at the catch of fish that they had taken; and so also were James and John, sons of Zebedee, who were partners with Simon. Then Jesus said to Simon, "Do not be afraid; from now on you will be catching people." When they had brought their boats to shore, they left everything and followed him.

LUKE 5:1–11

Jesus is speaking to the people. There are so many people that Jesus can't see them all well. He asks to sit in a boat to get a bit of distance so he can see all the people and they can see him.

Imagine Jesus in the boat. See the banks by the water filled with people. You are on the banks with the crowd. You hear Jesus preaching.

What is Jesus preaching about? Like he did on many occasions, he is preaching about the Kingdom. He is preaching about that entirely new way of being. Jesus is speaking of the Kingdom in which the poor are blessed, in which the gentle are blessed, in which the mourning are blessed, in which the peacemakers are blessed, in which those who hunger and thirst for justice are blessed, in which the persecuted are blessed, in which the pure of heart are blessed. (See Matthew 5:3–11.)

The Kingdom is where everything is turned upside down. Those who are marginal, those considered not respectable, are suddenly proclaimed as the people who are called to the Kingdom. The part of us that is weak, broken, or poor suddenly becomes the place where something new can begin. Jesus says, "Be in touch with your brokenness. Be in touch with your sinfulness. Turn to God because the Kingdom is close at hand. If you are ready to listen from your brokenness then something new can come forth in you."

When the sermon is over the people do what we often do; they say, "Now let's go and do what we were doing before. We know about this! We'd like to go on where we were." But Jesus says, "Throw out your nets for a catch."

He does not go back to his normal day-to-day living where everything is as it was before he started the sermon. He wants to move very concretely from the old way of being to the new way of being. But the disciples are still talking as they were talking before the sermon.

As we talk today.

At first they say, "Listen, Jesus, you are not a fisherman. You don't know how to fish. You are a preacher. We have been fishing all night and the night fish are usually closer to the surface than during the day, so if we didn't catch anything at night we are not going to catch anything during the day. It doesn't make any sense to try again. Can't you trust our judgment?" Then they say with a kind of grudging defeat, "If you say so. Okay, we'll do it."

The disciples respond with the normal logic. We see them do it all the time. Think about the story of the loaves and fish. Five loaves, two fish. Jesus says to his disciples, "Give the crowd five loaves of bread and two fish," and they say to Jesus, "Can't you count! Five loaves and two fish won't feed everyone!" And Jesus says, "Feed the multitude." (See Mark 6:38 and Matthew 14:17.)

Jesus says, "Throw out your nets," and they do. And they catch fish! But, interestingly, they do not catch as many fish as they need. They catch so many that they get embarrassed. It was the same thing with the loaves. Jesus doesn't say everyone should get a little piece of bread. No, there is so much bread left over that they don't know what to do with it. Here, in this story, their boats are filled so full they are embarrassed. They don't need so many fish! They would have been very happy with a normal catch.

Jesus breaks right through human logic. He's not interested. He is moving the whole reality to the Kingdom. Suddenly the disciples are no longer within the logic of the world. They have entered into the illogic of God. They are beyond all logic. They have entered into a whole new world. When Peter finally understands this, he doesn't say, "Lord, I was wrong. You do know how to fish." He says, "Lord, I am a sinful man." Peter's response is very beautiful because Peter senses he hadn't trusted in what was happening. He had heard the Lord speak about the Kingdom, about the new world order, but he realized he hadn't heard it at all. He hadn't taken it very seriously. He hadn't taken Jesus very seriously. But when the Lord breaks right through his logic, Peter says, "I am a sinful man. I haven't been willing to give you a chance. I was still doing my own thing, on my own terms, to get my little project done."

In the presence of the Kingdom, in the presence of that new reality, Peter understands that up until that point he was invested in himself. "Me, I want to catch fish. That is why I went out the whole night." He realizes that all that he was doing he did for himself.

Peter is not alone. The disciples constantly hear Jesus' stories from the perspective of power, from the perspective of the old world. You hear this all through the Gospel.

"Are you going to finally throw the Romans out and get some power going here?"

"Are you going to get this thing organized?"

Jesus breaks right through it and opens a whole new world. He says, "Follow me. Don't be afraid. I will make you catch people. I will introduce you to a completely new way of living and being" (Mark 1:17).

They leave everything behind and follow Jesus.

In our own lives, we hold on to our logic. Jesus

wants to break through it and open up a new way of being. We are afraid to let this happen to us because then we don't have control anymore. We don't have control over our future when we let Jesus enter into the center of our being.

We have to trust a direction for which we don't have a language. Jesus uses words like "breath," "life," "death," and "truth," but he imbues them with new meaning. The disciples don't understand and get confused. Only much later when the Spirit comes do the real meanings of these words become visible.

We Are Called

Jesus calls us to move away from the world of scarcity and from a way of thinking about scarcity, to a world of abundance and to a way of thinking about abundance. The disciples had a mentality of scarcity, and so do we. We think there is not enough for everyone so we have to be careful with what we have. We are fearful people. We are very afraid, and that fear creeps up on us in all kinds of ways.

We are afraid for ourselves. We are afraid of others. We are afraid of God. Fear is a pervasive quality in our lives. Fear makes us think in terms of scarcity. It makes us think, "This is a dangerous world. How am I going to survive? There is not enough for everyone. There is not enough food for everyone. There is not enough knowledge for everyone. There is not enough affection and I want to live! I want to be sure that I live! I want to stay alive!" This is a very common response in us.

When we are concerned that there isn't enough, our first response is to start hoarding. We start hoarding the bread, the fish. Hoarding honor. Hoarding affection, hoarding knowledge. Hoarding ideas.

If we start hoarding we find ourselves with enemies.

There are always people who will say, "You have much more than me." You might say, "I know, but I need it for emergency situations." They respond, "But I need it now. I am hungry now." "I want to know this now." "I want to build this now."

If we think with a scarcity mentality we find ourselves with enemies who want to take some of what we have hoarded. We are more and more afraid, because the more we have, the more people want our surplus. The more surplus we have, the more we are going to build walls around what we have hoarded.

The higher the walls get, the more fear we have of the enemies we imagine outside the walls. We start building bombs to protect us from our imagined enemies, and then we get scared of the bombs that our enemies might build in retaliation. We find ourselves in a prison that we built ourselves because of a fear that comes out of a mentality of scarcity. Of not having enough.

Think about it. How do you hold on to things?

Like holding on to a relationship, for instance.

"This is my friend. I am not going to invite him

because the others will like him more than they like me and I don't want to be alone."

You are holding on to that friend and not letting go. Scarcity mentality is very visible in the Gospel. Jesus is saying that God is the God of abundance. Wherever Jesus appears there is not only life but life to the full.

Jesus comes to bring life, and life to the full. He brings much more than we even ask for. Jesus always offers us something beyond our expectations. The reality that Jesus keeps promising is a reality that we can't even grasp. He speaks about eternal life, the truth, the light, the life.

Jesus' miracles are signs of a new reality. He says, "Do you remember how much bread was left over? You still don't believe?" Jesus gets almost desperate and says, "How can I make you believe that you can trust me? How can I make you believe that with me you will not lack for anything?" Even after the resurrection, the disciples don't grasp the new reality. Peter says, "Let's go back fishing. The Lord is gone. It's all over." They are back fishing and suddenly they see a figure on the shore and the person calls out, "Did you catch anything?" And they say, "No, we didn't." "Well, throw out your nets again on the left side." They do, and suddenly they have all this fish. John turns to Peter and says, "It is the Lord." Peter then jumps into the sea and makes his way toward Jesus (John 21:7).

The Lord gives more than we can deal with. That is what finally makes the disciples see. Even though the disciples can't fully understand what it all means, the signs are so powerful that, indeed, they finally leave their nets and follow.

Following Jesus, as described in the Gospels, is first of all an invitation to follow the Lord of abundance. We are invited to follow the Lord even if we can't fully absorb the enormousness of this divine hospitality.

I hope you see what I am saying. Fear is precisely what makes us hold on to our position and possessions. It makes us hold on to what we have, because we are so afraid we will lose what we need. Love is overcoming fear. Love is letting go and trusting that in the letting go life will multiply. Life will become *more*.

"Follow me. Let go of your logic. Let go of your way of thinking. Let go of your fears and trust that something new will happen. You will enter into the Kingdom of abundance, of joy, of peace, of freedom." We say, "Yes, but listen. Let's not go too quickly. Let's work it out. Let's see what we are in for."

We don't quite trust.

Jesus says, "Follow me. Look at me. Didn't you see the fish? Didn't you see the bread? You still have all your arguments. You are still fighting. You feel unhappy. You are not content. You are afraid. You are in a prison that you built yourself. You are worried, and I say, 'Follow me,' and you are still arguing." We say, "I don't know if I can let go. I know the fear I have and I don't know the love."

We know the pain. We are less familiar with the

love. What do we do? We choose the pain. We hold on to our ways because we don't know what it would mean to let them go. "Follow me" means "Let go of those fears." Jesus says, "Think about the Kingdom first and all the other things you are so worried about will fall into place. Why are you so worried? Why are you so preoccupied? Why are you so afraid? I would like to make you free. I would like you to follow the Lord in whose presence there is life. I want to give you life. If you hold on to your own things you get enemies. You get walls. You get death. There is destruction, war, and violence. But I am the Lord of life. Choose life! Choose me in whose presence there is abundance!"

How Do We Respond?

By letting go, by giving away! Five loaves, two fish. They multiply in the giving. There is enough for everyone. What we hold on to always diminishes. What we give away always multiplies. It is the great illogic. The poor will possess the land. Those who give away what they have will see it multiply. Those who hold on to it in fear will see it dwindle right in front of them.

This happens in my life. If I hold on to a friend or if I hold on to an idea, I find myself anxious and nervous. Why do I choose this? Do something different! Something happens. Something totally new.

Our response to the call to follow Jesus can be very concrete. Our response is to take small steps away from "me" and "my fears" toward the Lord.

Following does not require dramatic gestures.

I am amazed by the number of people who ask the big questions when they already know the small answers. Some people ask me, "Should I really leave it all behind and go on a mission? Is that what Jesus is asking?" "Do I really need to leave my family and my career and give up all my possessions to follow Jesus?" I respond, "Why ask the big questions when you could simply say, 'I promise not to yell at my baby. I promise to make a little step.'"

The great secret of the spiritual life is that you already know the little steps, even if you don't know the big ones. You don't need to know the big steps to take the little steps. You only have to take one step at a time. The interesting thing is that the person who is in touch with the Lord knows what those little steps are. For example, we could say, "I am not going to speak about that person that way anymore. I am not going to gossip." It is a little thing. Nobody notices. We still don't like that person, but at least we are not going to say bad things about them anymore. Little step. The next step might be that we smile at them. Then we invite them over. Before we know it we are friends. If we look back we see it was a long journey of little steps.

All the great people in history started with little

steps. St. Francis of Assisi didn't suddenly rip off his clothes and move to a cave. It was four years of struggling and taking little steps. He asked himself, "What should I think?" "How should I act?" He worked it out in little steps. We focus on the dramatic end of it all, but that is not what I want you to pay attention to. Focus on the small steps he took to get there.

Be very aware. You know exactly what you have to do tonight. You also know what you have to do tomorrow. You also know what you don't need to do. You have to trust that if you take these steps of faithfulness in your thinking, in your speaking, in your acting, you can make a long trip with small steps. You will hear the call louder and louder and know where you are going.

I don't want to make it sound too easy.

Somehow we must trust that all the steps we need to take are close at hand. Jesus doesn't ask us to jump. He asks us first to move, very, very carefully, step by step by step.

The first step is to listen.

The second is to step away from "mine." When making decisions we can ask ourselves, "Am I doing this out of fear for my survival or can I act in trust?" We will know when we are acting out of fear and when we are acting out of love. Always choose love. Do not act out of fear. Again it is small changes: don't say or think things because you're scared. Thinking thoughts of fear leads to more fear.

Following Jesus is moving away from fear and toward love. Always toward the Lord.

It is crucial that we step away from fear and toward the One who is Love (1 John 4:8). We must keep our eyes on the Lord of abundance. Jesus is the one who promises life, and life to the full. He doesn't say, "I am going to make life difficult for you." He talks about detachment and letting go, but that is only later. First of all, he speaks about moving toward life. He says, "Follow me and keep your eyes on that place that promises you life to the full."

Use prayer and meditation to keep your eyes on that place of life.

If you want to develop the spiritual life keep the Lord in your mind. Look at him.

St. Ignatius of Loyola would say, "See him, hear him, touch him, taste him, smell him." Be fully present and become familiar. Always stay close to the invitation "Come and see," because if you really see, if you really look around, and you really become familiar with the beauty of Jesus, you will see that the beauty of this person is his invitation to love. It is an invitation to go where he calls. Then it will be easy.

Perhaps "easy" is not quite the right word. It is something we do because we are *attracted* to it. The spiritual life is not giving up something. It is first of all following the One. It is not first of all letting go of all fears. It is first of all being led to love. If we keep the Lord, his Kingdom, his Word, and his Gospel in our mind, if this becomes our inner space, we will know what to do because we have that world around us. We are in the House of the Lord. We are there with God and somehow we are in the right space to make decisions because our eyes are focused. We know the beauty of God and we want to be there. We have real desire.

We all have our unique vocation. We all have a call to follow. It is exciting to trust in our call.

Do not dramatize it. Listen, and you will know what your next move is. You will experience a desire to do it because it is always a move from fear to love.

"Come. Come follow me."

FOLLOWING JESUS IS following the voice of the One who calls us away from useless wandering or from just sitting there. Jesus says, "Follow me." If we choose to listen and follow, our life gradually comes into focus. It is no longer tiring. We know where to direct our energies. We know what is important and what is not. Following Jesus means to let go of the "I" and move toward the "other." Following Jesus means to dare to move out of ourselves and to slowly let go of building our "self" up. It means to be guided by the other who draws us into an entirely new way of being.

Following does not mean imitating or copying

someone's behavior. I think that sometimes we end up imitating or saying as he or she says, or doing as she or he does. But following Jesus is something other than imitating or copying his way of doing things.

It is important for us to see this distinction. If we imitate someone we are not developing a personal, intimate relationship with that person. We imitate the person whom we look up to or the person whom we admire and are not close to.

Sometimes imitation has a quality of fear to it.

"I am afraid that he or she doesn't like me, so I am going to imitate what he or she does so that I am acceptable."

There is no inner space there.

Imitating someone can also come from laziness.

"I am going to do what he or she does, but I am not going to get involved."

Somebody who imitates another person doesn't really get involved with that person. They don't want an encounter from within.

In contrast, when we speak about following Jesus we speak about a movement that comes from our heart. It comes from the deepest place of our person. It has something to do with our innermost self. Following Jesus means to live our life in his spirit, in his light, in his heart, but with our spirit, with our light, and with our heart. It doesn't mean that we become passive imitators. No, it means that we become persons who discover our own vocation, our own unique call, in a whole new way.

To follow Jesus means to give our unique form and incarnation to God's love.

To follow Jesus means to live our lives as authentically as he lived his. It means to give away our ego and to follow the God of Love as Jesus shows us. Following Jesus requires a conversion. It requires a new heart and a new mind.

There are no two followers of Jesus who are the same. Look at the great variety of saints. They all have their own unique style of discipleship. One of the most exciting aspects of the Christian life is that it does not put people in a mold, but creates a rich variety of people in whom the love of God becomes incarnate in very different ways.

If following were imitating then there could never be a community. A community is precisely a gathering of those who in different ways have integrated and incorporated the call. The vitality of the Christian community exists precisely because there are so many ways of following Jesus.

We all reflect God's love in different ways. Together we are like a mosaic. In a mosaic one stone is bright, another stone is gold, another stone is small. If we look at it closely we can admire the beauty of each stone, but if we step back from it, we can see that all the little stones reveal a beautiful picture and tell a story that none

of the stones can tell by itself. Together the different
stones reflect the face of God to the world.

To follow Jesus is to hear his call as a very personal
call. It is a call to give a unique witness to the love of
God as revealed in Jesus. There are many ways of being
disciples so that the fullness of God's love is visible in
the Christian community. For some, this means a call
to radical poverty. For others, it means faithfulness in
marriage. For others, it means a life of service in the
secular world. For others, it is a life of contemplation
and hiddenness. Whatever our personal response is, it
is a response of love. It is a way of giving visibility to
God's love. Every disciple reflects something special of
God's love.

Discipleship—giving expression to God's love—
takes many forms. Some people are passionate lovers.
Others have an indignant love. They see injustice and
immediately go to it. Others have a very gentle love.
They radiate welcoming. Wherever they are they create community. There are others with a quiet love that
is very hidden.

These are all forms of love, and we each have our
own way. God's love is so rich and broad that it takes
many people to make it visible. The many forms of love
support each other.

Lord Jesus,

I come to you to enter into the mystery of your way—the way of discipleship, the way that leads from the cross to new life. It is not an easy way, but it is a way of peace and joy. Help me to be here with a heart open to suffering, a mind open to understanding, and a will ready to follow.

There are many struggles and I will always have many struggles, but with you, O Lord, I am living in the Light. With you, O Lord, I am moving more and more toward life. With you, O Lord, I know I am safe.

Let me celebrate my life in a spirit of gratitude. Grateful that I am here and grateful you are my God.

AMEN

✳

THE CHALLENGE

"Love Your Enemies"

"Love your enemies, do good to those who hate you, bless those who curse you, and pray for those who treat you badly. To the one who slaps you on one cheek, present to them the other one too. If someone takes your cloak, do not refuse your tunic. Give to everyone who asks you, and do not ask for your property back from the one who robs you. Treat others as you would like them to treat you. If you love those who love you, what thanks can you expect? Even sinners love those who love them. And if you do good to those who do good to you, what thanks can you expect, for even sinners do that much. And if you lend to those from whom you hope to receive, what thanks can you expect? Even sinners lend to sinners, expecting to get back the same amount. Instead love your enemies and do good, and lend without any hope of return. You will have a great reward and be sons and daughters of the Most High, for God himself is kind to the ungrateful and the wicked."

LUKE 6:27–35

"Love your enemies" is probably the call that is most central to the whole Christian message. It touches precisely that place where the New Testament is really new. It is an idea that breaks through history through Jesus. It is a challenge that Jesus presents to us. But we have a very poor and somewhat distorted view of what love is. To talk about loving our enemies, we must first speak about loving our friends.

Love

When I think about how I live my life, and how others live theirs, I am amazed by how enormously needy I am. I am in need of affection. I am in need of attention. I am in need of affirmation. I am in need of praise. I am in need of influence, power, and success. I sense how strong these needs are in me and how strong they are in others.

They are, in fact, so strong that often we find ourselves setting up our lives to satisfy them. There is a tragic quality to living this way. You might have noticed it yourself. As soon as a need is satisfied we discover it is not enough. As soon as we get the praise that we prayed for and someone says, "You are the most beautiful person I have ever met," we think to ourselves, "Is that really true? Does she say that to everyone?" Or if someone says, "You are wonderful. That thing you did, the movie you produced, the paper you wrote is fantastic," it creates anxiety, because now we have to live up to an expectation. People become more and more nervous the more famous they are. They are afraid to lose what they have carefully built up.

I spent time in San Francisco and Los Angeles with filmmakers and people who were in show business. I was amazed at how everyone was in constant need of hearing how great they were. It seemed like there was no end to that need. If you told them they were great it was never enough. Even people who were at the top of their success, who had won Oscars and other prizes, were still not happy. They had still not received enough affirmation. You say to them, "You are the greatest of all!" and they say, "You say that today, but what about tomorrow?"

Even people who are immensely praised and have made an enormous amount of money, who have awards, success, and applause, can be deeply depressed. If you get closer and you prick the balloon, you realize they are just as insecure as everyone else. Underneath all that wealth, all that success, and all that praise, they are still a little person who asks, "Do you love me?"

We hear about people who die by suicide at the top

of their careers. You ask, "How could that happen? They are rich, famous, and successful," and you realize that he or she was living in a way that was so tense that it became unbearable.

Our needs are enormous. The need for affection and success is very deep for many people. It is amazing how strong it is. I often wonder if people really like me and if they like what I am doing. It's awful! I can't get away from it. I give a sermon about humility and the first question I ask myself is whether people liked it!

Why are we so needy?

Where does the neediness come from?

It comes from an experience of woundedness. We are wounded people. We have been wounded in such a way that we question our worth. We have doubts about ourselves. We ask, "Am I worthy of being?" "Am I making a contribution to the human family?" "Am I part of anything?"

We might not express it this way, but somewhere we feel rejected. Somewhere very deep we feel we are not quite acceptable. We point to our mother, father, brother, church, or school and say, "I am so angry about what happened to me," "I am still struggling for self-respect because my father always put me down," "My mother didn't have a great affection for me because she liked her other children more than me," "The church made me feel bad about myself."

Out of that feeling of woundedness we become very needy. We are desperately looking for that final feeling of being okay. We have a deep feeling that we are not acceptable. We point to certain events or people to blame while we know in our hearts that there is another explanation.

There is a problem with this need. It can become violent. Our loneliness, our self-doubt, and our inner anguish can be so great that we try to force people to love us. "Please love me. Please tell me that I am okay." Then, what is meant to be an expression of affection can become demanding. In a world where people are so in need of affirmation they can start grabbing, biting, slapping, and hitting out of their need. Prisons are full of people who committed crimes just to get attention, even if it is the most negative kind.

Our needs can lead to wounds. We can wound people with our needs because we often force people to give something they do not have. We force people to be God for us. When we make other people into God we become demons ourselves. That is where the struggle is. Needs lead to wounds and the wounds create new needs, and on and on it goes. If we ask, "Where do my needs come from?" we realize that our wounds come from someone in the past who hurt us because that other person was so needy.

In response, we might say, "I am not going to do anything with my needs in that way." We don't want to hurt anybody. But before we know it, our children say, "I feel unseen by you." Or our friends say, "I am disappointed in you." Or our partner says, "You don't give me all I really need. After so many years of marriage there is still this unfulfilled place between us." There is enormous pain, because the people who feel hurt by us are those we love deeply. Somehow we couldn't avoid it. We feel sad about it. We see that the interlocking network of wounds and needs goes into the future too.

But what exactly is the wound we experience?

Rejection. The wound is the experience of not being fully loved. A wounded person is a person who deeply in his or her heart doesn't know that he or she is truly loved.

The words of Jesus speak directly to this human condition. Jesus wants to free us from the chain that imprisons us. He wants to free us by revealing that we are loved before we can give or receive love from anybody. Jesus came to reveal to us the first love. The original love. We are called by Jesus to come in touch with that first love.

The first love says, "I loved you before you could love anyone or before you could receive love from anyone. I have accepted you. You are accepted. You are loved no matter what mother, father, brother, sister, school, church, society does. You are born out of my love. I have breathed you out of my love. I have spoken you out of my love. You are the incarnation of my love and in me there is no hatred, there is no revenge, there is no resentment. There is nothing that wants to reject you. I love you. Can you trust that love?"

The original love is the original blessing.

The original love is the original acceptance.

Long before we talk about original sin or original rejection we should speak of God's original love.

It is God's love that allows us to love one another. It is that first love that is the basis for all creative human relationships. It is that love that we want to make visible to each other, among each other, and with each other.

Jesus said, "Love one another because I have loved you first."

The whole spiritual life is a life where we come in touch with that first love. As soon as we touch that place of the first love we begin to slowly become free from the chain of needs and wounds that holds us imprisoned.

The spiritual life is really a life that wants to make us free. Free to love.

Jesus meets the woman who pours ointment on his feet and wipes them with her hair. Jesus says she must have been forgiven because she loves so much (Luke 7:36–48). What this means is that she has understood how much she is loved, and this knowledge has set her free to love Jesus with all her heart.

When we come in touch with the first love we come in touch with that center of our being where we feel totally loved without condition or limits. When we come in touch with the first love we are free to love people without asking for anything in return.

That is not what worldly love is all about. Worldly

love is a transaction. The transactional quality of worldly love is precisely why people are always in trouble. If they give something they expect something in return. This is where the conflicts come from. This is where the hostility comes from. This is where the anger, jealousy, resentment, and revenge come from. This understanding of love is where the whole human chaos comes from.

Jesus says, "Give without expecting anything in return" (Luke 6:34–35).

Jesus doesn't want us to be masochists who do nice things for others and say, "Oh no, you don't have to give anything back. I'll just be miserable about it."

No. Jesus says, "You are loved so much that you don't even have to think about little returns."

How do we know this love?

Through prayer. We have to pray in order to let the first love touch us so that we can know it again.

We pray to know not only in our head, but in our heart, and in the center of our being that we are fully loved. That is why we pray. We pray so we can walk around this world and not be so needy, not be wounding others, and not be giving so we can get something in return. We pray to be free.

If we really hear this, if we can really feel this somewhere in our guts,* then we are really getting some-

---

* Nouwen uses the word "guts" in the Greek meaning of the word. In Greek, *splagchnizomai* means to be moved as to one's

where, because this is, I think, where Jesus is most challenging.

Following Jesus means to live a life in which we start loving one another with God's original love and not with the needy and wounded love that harms others. Original love is a love that has the power to love enemies as well as friends. It is a divine love that makes us "sons and daughters of the Most High, who is kind to the grateful and the wicked . . . who causes the sun to rise on bad people as well as the good, and the rain to fall on honest and dishonest people" (Matthew 5:45).

How do we participate in this divine love?

Let's try to answer that by exploring some ideas about marriage, friendship, and community. I sense that for many people their interpersonal relationships are what count the most but can also be what can cause the most harm.

Love of Friends

Marriage often goes like this: "I love you. You love me. I feel very attracted to you. Let's get together. We really are quite compatible. Why don't we try to live together and maybe we can form a team. Maybe we can even get married."

---

bowels, hence to be moved with compassion, have compassion (for the bowels were thought to be the seat of love and pity).

After several years, one of you says, "I really want to get to know you. I still have this feeling that you haven't let me know all about yourself." The other person might say, "I am trying really hard and I have shared all I have to share. I have given all I have to give." And the other says, "I am feeling quite lonely with you. Somehow you are not taking our marriage seriously enough." Then stresses and tension increase and one of you says, "Well, maybe we should have a little distance." Then one of you says, "Let's try again. We should ask for some help . . ."

There is a kind of hopelessness to this kind of love. We cling to one another and our demands become oppressive and desperate.

We tend to think that love begins and ends with our interpersonal relationships. This is not true according to scripture. Love of others begins with our relationship with God.

We can love others because the "I" in our innermost self has heard the first love—which is God's unconditional, unlimited love. When we come together in relationships, we recognize that others are also loved with the first love. The first love incarnates in different ways in every person and calls us together to build a new home, a new community, a new dwelling place for God in this world. This is what marriage is all about. This is what friendship is about. This is what community is about. True relationships among people point to God.

Scripture tells us that human relationships, whether in friendship, marriage, or community, mean that two people discover that they belong to a love that is greater than each of them can contain and to which they both point.

Relationships point away from ourselves to the larger love that embraces us. In marriage we say, "We have a bond together not just because we have a good interpersonal relationship, but because we have recognized that God has called us together as a new way of making God's love visible in this world. By coming together and building a home we can receive new people, we can be hospitable. We can create space for children, for friends. It is a space that points to the One who calls us together."

Marriage is not that two people love each other so much that they can find God in each other, but that God loves them so much that they can discover each other as living reminders of God's presence.

Marriage is the mystery that God loves us so much that we can discover together how God's presence can be made visible here and now by our commitment to each other. Our faithfulness becomes possible not because we stay the same or stay together, not because we are compatible or that we have the same life goals, but because God holds us together in that first love.

Let me try to say it differently. Love, as Jesus reveals it to us, is a relationship between persons. The word "person" is a wonderful word. It comes from the Latin words *per*, which means "through," and *sonare*, which means "to sound." A person is someone who is sounding through.

What are we sounding through? We are sounding through a greater love than we ourselves can contain. When we say to somebody, "I love you," that really means, "You are a window through which I can get a glimpse of the infinite love of God." If we say, "I really love you," it doesn't mean that the person gives us all that we need; it means, "You bring me in touch with the God that I have already met in the depth of my heart. You are sounding through to me the love that I have in my heart. I am sounding through for you the love you already recognize in your heart." This is really what all intimate relationships are about.

Love between a man and a woman, between a man and a man, between a woman and a woman, and between people in communities is a love among persons who are sounding through God's infinite, unlimited, unconditional love. We broken, limited persons are windows on the unlimited, unconditional, unbroken, perfect love of God.

Some people say, "You have to see God in the other," or "You must see God in the world." I don't think we can see God in the world. I, Henri Nouwen, can't see anything! However, if I have discovered God in my heart and God in my solitude, then the God in me can discover the God in you. It is a whole different way of seeing. We discover that we are both loved by the same God and can come together to celebrate that love in whatever way God calls us.

If we know that first love, if we dwell in the House of God, then the presence of God in us can recognize the presence of God in the other. Conversely, if we have a demon in our heart we will see demons all around us. If we have dark forces in us, we will see dark forces all over the place. People with a dark heart see other people with a dark heart. Darkness speaks to darkness. Evil speaks to evil. But love speaks to love and God speaks to God.

The Christian life—following Jesus in a life of discipleship—is about discovering how God's presence can be made visible here and now by our love for each other. Friendship, marriage, and community are all different ways to reveal to one another the original, all-embracing love of God.

Love of Enemies

It has been said that the love of enemies is the criterion of holiness. It's true. If we love our enemies we are on the way to holiness. Staretz Silouan (1866–1938), one of the famous orthodox monks living on Mt. Athos in Greece, kept saying that. He said, "If you pray for your enemies peace will come to you, and when you love your enemies take for certain that Grace brings Divine Love to you."

Love of enemies is a dominant characteristic of Jesus' life. Remember what he said on the cross: "Father, forgive them; for they do not know what they do" (Luke 23:34). Remember St. Stephen, the first martyr of Christianity, who in death asked God to forgive his enemies. He said, "Lord, do not hold this sin against them" (Acts 7:60). Speaking words of forgiveness is where the love of enemies becomes visible.

What is an enemy?

An enemy is someone we have defined as being against us in contrast to someone who is for us. Many of us have a strange need to divide the world up into people who are for us and those who are against us.

Even more strange is that our identity is often dependent on having enemies. We don't exist without an enemy. We define ourselves by what we are opposed to. We define the enemy and the enemy is there to define us.

This kind of self-identity is built on the great illusion that we are what people say to us or what people do to us. The great illusion is that our identity, our selfhood, depends on our friends and our enemies, on those who like us and those who don't like us. This is the great lie.

The good news of the Gospel is that God has no enemies. The Gospel tells us that God loves every human being the same way and with the same intensive love. God's love touches "not only the good but the wicked" (1 Peter 2:18). "The rain falls on those who are good and those who are bad." God does not make distinctions. God's love is universal.

We Are Challenged

It is very important for us to realize that if we indeed want to love one another with God's love and not with our wounded, needy love, then we are called to make our enemies, again and again and again, into friends.

Enemies are enemies by the way we exclude them from the love of God. When we love with God's love we can no longer divide people into those who deserve God's love and those who don't. When we come to know God's first love nobody can be excluded from that love.

Martin Luther King, Jr., said, "Love is the only force capable of transforming an enemy into a friend . . . By its very nature, love creates and builds up." He said, "Yes, it is love that will save our world and our civilization, love even for enemies."

Abraham Lincoln said, "Do I not destroy my enemies when I make them my friends?"

These are very powerful words.

Indeed, we are called to love our fellow human beings with a divine love, with the love of God. "Be perfect as your heavenly Father is perfect" (Matthew 5:48).

"If you love those who love you, what thanks can you expect? Even sinners love those who love them. Instead love your enemies and do good, and lend without any hope of return" (Luke 6:32–35).

Love people as God loves. We can do this when we are solidly rooted in our own love, which is God's love.

Notice for a moment that the enemy is the one who finally destroys us. Hating the enemy costs us. We often allow the enemy to have power over us.

I have noticed in my own life that people I don't like have power over me because I am always thinking about them. They preoccupy me and have control over my thinking. I find myself jealous, resentful, and vengeful. I lose peace. I am holding on to these people as my enemies.

Loving our enemies is the way of becoming free of our enemies. We free ourselves by letting go, by loving them, by caring for them.

One of the most beautiful things is that when we let the enemy go out of our heart by love and forgiveness, we are suddenly free to let that unlimited, all-embracing love of God pour into us. We become a new person every time we forgive an enemy, because we let go of the angry person inside who was holding on to fear.

The core of our faith is to be free people—free from the power we give to our enemies, free to love every human being with the divine love that always forgives, seven times seven and seven again.

The enemy remains the enemy only as long as we have not yet fully seen the love of God. Feelings of hatred, rejection, jealousy, and resentment enslave us in our self-made prison of fear. We become the victims of our self-made enemy. But every time we are able to forgive, and no longer define ourselves over and against the other, we enter deep into the House of God, which is the House of Love. Love of enemies becomes the way to knowing God as the God of the first love.

How Can We Respond to Jesus' Challenge to Love Our Enemies?

There are two very concrete things we can do.

Pray for your enemies.

People are not all that interested in praying for people they don't like. But try it! Pray for people that you do not like. You really have to work at it.

"Jesus, I pray for him whom I can't stand at all."

The enemy is an internal presence, so we are dealing with something very intimate to us.

It is very important. Go to prayer and pray. Pray for

your enemies because when you do you are acting out God's love.

Prayers for our enemy can open the way to a new divine knowledge of the basic unity of the human family.

Do concrete acts of forgiveness and service.

Members of the Christian community, whether it is in marriage or friendship or larger communities, can stay together if they can confess and forgive as a way of life.

Do not wait until you feel better about things. No! You should do it precisely when you don't feel better. Act ahead of the feelings. Do not let emotions decide what you are going to do.

We have a knowledge of God's love. We know that God loves this person as much as God loves us. We know that God loves this person as intimately as us. We may not believe it, but it doesn't matter. We are making concrete actions of forgiveness even when our feelings are ambivalent.

Return to the knowledge of the first love that was there before your feelings got hurt. The act of forgiveness will shake your whole life.

What words do we choose when we speak to a person we don't like? We are still filled with anger and hurt, but we say a few things to him or her that indicate our desire to restore connection with them even when we don't get anything in return. We know that God loves

this person as much as God loves us. Let's remind ourselves of that truth, that true revelation. This is where
loving our enemy starts.

Loving our enemies starts with small, concrete, par-
ticular actions in the direction of our knowledge. It does
not start in the direction of our feelings. We can act according to what we know. We know that God loves us.
We can trust our knowledge and eventually our feelings will catch up. The feelings follow our knowledge.
In a world where feelings have become so dominant this
is an important spiritual truth to remember.

Let us think about it. How can we begin to grow in
God's love and love one another with that divine love?

FOLLOWING JESUS IS a movement away from "just
wandering around" or "just sitting there." A lot of us
live a life in which we do a lot of wandering—physical
wandering or mental wandering—in many directions,
or we sit there not knowing what to do with our life.
There is a certain fatigue there. Following Jesus means
moving in the right direction. Suddenly we know where
we are going, and our lives take on a more regular pat-
tern and we have more focus.

Following Jesus also means something other than
being drawn into a movement, even a good one. It can
be a very good movement because we can find some

help there for our emotional life. But following Jesus is not just about finding a way to handle our emotions or our self. It is a different movement. It is in fact a letting go of our worldly self to find our true self in Jesus.

And contrary to popular opinion we are not called to imitate Jesus. We are called to form a community of people who through different ways reflect the great love of Jesus. Not one of us can reflect the fullness of that love. Therefore following Jesus means something different for each of us. There are many forms and shapes in this pursuit. The exciting thing about Christian community is that we have so many ways to be a disciple; we can be an activist or a contemplative. We can embody both. There are different ways we can live out God's love. Some of us are very passionate, others are more quiet and hardly noticeable.

Following Jesus does not mean to be carried by Jesus either. Following Jesus does not mean that Jesus picks us up from the ground. Oftentimes we say, "I follow Jesus, so everything is fine," or "I have prayed to Jesus and you'll be fine." But, as many of us know, it's not that simple.

Sometimes there is an eagerness in us, or around us, to turn Jesus into a problem solver. We think he will solve all our problems, and if all our problems are not solved we don't have enough faith. That is not really Jesus' intent. At least that is not what is in the Gospel. Jesus is not there to get us out of hot water. He is not the cure-all for our difficulties. Jesus is not the end of the hard times in our lives. That is not what Jesus is.

To follow Jesus means that *we* do the walking. *We* are the ones doing the talking, living life, getting involved. *We* are the ones struggling, the ones who need to work hard. Jesus, in a way, does not take away the difficulties of our journey. I even dare to say that, following Jesus means everything changes while everything remains the same. You know very well that followers of Jesus—disciples—are people who live real human lives. The work of life does not come easier to them because they are disciples.

Life, as many of us know, can actually become more difficult—more painful—when we choose to follow Jesus. Yet at the same time we gain a certain strength because we no longer live our life or our agony alone. We no longer live our struggle in isolation. We no longer live our pains as if nobody cares. Indeed, following Jesus means walking in his path, taking steps behind the One who shows us the way in our dark, broken, painful world.

Following Jesus means to live our life in companionship with the One who understands us fully. "Companion," from the Old French *compaignon*, literally means "one who breaks bread with another," based on the Latin *com*, "together with," and *panis*, "bread."

Following Jesus means a life in communion, with a guide.

It makes an enormous difference whether we struggle alone or together. To know that our life is still a struggle but no longer a lonely struggle is a new experience entirely. Following Jesus makes life very different and very new.

When we walk with Jesus we can know that we have a fellow traveler, someone-with-us. Jesus is God-with-us, the one we can trust with our whole life, the one who shows us the way.

Lord Jesus,

Free me from the many things that occupy and preoccupy me. Help me just to be with you. To pray with you, glorify you, thank you, worship you. I want to be attentive, more ready to hear you, more willing to understand the mystery of your birth and life, your dying and your rising. Make me still, Lord, make me quiet, and speak to me in that silence.

AMEN

CHAPTER FOUR

THE COST
"Take Up Your Cross"

"Come to me, all you that are weary and are carrying heavy burdens, and I will give you rest. Take my yoke upon you, and learn from me; for I am gentle and humble in heart, and you will find rest for your souls. For my yoke is easy, and my burden is light."

MATTHEW 11:28–30

All that exists, heaven and earth, was created by God's word. There is nothing that is not spoken by God. God has spoken the Word and through the Word of God everything has life.

All that exists is created by the Word of God. God has spoken to us.

The Word of God—Jesus—became flesh, became one among us, living in a small town in a small country, somewhere on one of the planets in our solar system.

The Word through which all is created became a person called Jesus.

What this means is so beautifully expressed by St. Paul when he says that Jesus Christ, the Word of God, did not cling to his divine privileges of being the One in whom all is created, but emptied himself and became as one of us. And more than that, he not only became as one of us, but he was obedient to death, a death on the cross.

God in whom all is created stripped himself of his divinity. That is, he didn't cling to divine privileges; he chose to become One among us. He was One who wanted to live our life to the full extent of what that means. That is, One who wanted to die with us. One that wanted to experience our human condition in the body. One that wanted to go with us to the absurdity of death.

Death is so absurd. Who of us can really grasp it? We want life and yet there is a certainty of death. God wanted to enter with us into that absurdity of death and feel the human condition more fully and more totally than we ourselves can.

He made it visible by dying the most absurd death. The Holy One nailed naked on a cross between two criminals. That is the unspeakable mystery that we as Christians believe.

But do we really?

God in whom all is created was hung as if he were a sinner on the cross. He is cast out and destroyed. And, in that way, God became more deeply united with humanity than we ourselves can believe.

I want you to hear this one sentence. It is very important. It comes from the Gospel of John. "When I am lifted up from the earth," Jesus says (as on the cross and also as lifted up in the resurrection), "I shall draw all people to myself" (John 12:32). This means that the divine movement of death and resurrection is a movement in which all human flesh has been lifted up. It means that all humanity has been drawn into that mystery of Christ's death and resurrection. It means that in Jesus' death all human mortality, brokenness, illness, sickness, confusion, agony, and loneliness have been embraced. It means that there is no human being anywhere in the world who is not lifted up on the cross with Jesus.

If it is true that Jesus on the cross is the Word in whom all is created, then we are all lifted up with Christ on the cross. All of human flesh—whether we are children, teenagers, young adults, mature people, elderly people; whether we are from the United States, Russia, Asia, Africa, Ireland, Nicaragua; whether we are prisoners or free people; whether we are people at war or people at peace; whether we are poor people or rich people—are all lifted up in that event on Golgotha. Not just people of this world here and now, but also the people of the generations, people from the centuries before Christ and also centuries ahead of us, of which we don't know the end. All the people—past, present, and future—have been lifted up in that mystery of Christ's death and resurrection.

All of humanity has been nailed on the cross. There is no suffering, whether it is loneliness, anger, pain, or rejection, that has not been suffered by God. Because of that, we, with our anger, with our pain, with our struggles, are in God and lifted up through the death and resurrection of Jesus. The Risen Lord is the Lord in whose body we have been gathered. All of humanity.

There is great hope in this understanding. This is the secret to seeing Jesus as the manifestation of God's compassion.

Do you know where the word "compassion" comes from? It comes from the Latin *com*, which means "with," and *passio*, "to suffer." "To suffer with" is compassion. Jesus manifests to us that God is a God who suffers with all of us. There is no human suffering in you or anyone else in the world that has not been suffered by God. Consolation begins with this knowing. God is suffering all human suffering.

In the Old Testament the Hebrew word for compassion is *rachuwm*. That word is taken from the root word *rechem*, which means "womb." God, hence, is a mother who suffers the suffering of her children in her womb.

In the Gospel, in the original Greek, when Jesus says he had pity, the text really says he had compassion. He felt the agony and pain of the people in his guts, in his viscera, in his interior organs. He suffered so deeply, he was so moved, that when he saw the widow of Nain and her child who was to be buried, he had compassion (Luke 7:11–17). He experienced the agony and pain of this mother, this widow, this lonely woman, so deeply that he raised the child from the dead. His compassion became a movement of life.

The great event in Nain is not so important because Jesus performed a miracle. The great event is that Jesus felt the suffering of that woman—*as deeply as that woman herself felt it*—and therefore it became a movement, a movement of life. It was a suffering with this woman in unity that was life-giving and that brought the child back again as a gift to his mother.

God's compassion for all human suffering is exactly what becomes visible on the cross. What this means is that we are called to see God's suffering in the people. Every time we see someone in pain and we wonder how that person is going to live through it, know that God suffered that pain and is suffering that pain with that person. In a way, the whole of history is the showing of the depth of God's suffering. From a Christian perspective, history is the unfolding of the intensity and immensity of God's suffering, but also of God's resurrection, because in the midst of all the suffering, you can see signs of hope again and again and again.

Our Cross

If we follow the news in the morning we might wonder how anyone can eat their breakfast and go to work.
There is so much pain in all the reports. I think to myself, "If I take this really seriously how can I ever do
anything?" I hear about war, famine, terrorism, and
environmental disasters, and I think, "If I focus too
much on this, how can I live?" Sometimes the only way
to survive is to become numb and say, "I can't pay attention to all that. It is too much. It is beyond my control. I've got my own problems."

Or there is anger. If, for example, on Sunday morning the minister talks about all the problems of the world
and all week long we have been hearing about them, and
then on Sunday morning they are there again, we feel
powerless. "What do you want us to do about it?" We get
upset, nervous, and angry, and it doesn't help anyone and
often leads to inaction on our part. We might even want
to shout, "Why can't you say some nice things instead?"

Confrontation with human suffering does not lead
to compassion. It leads to anger, numbness, irritation,
and rejection, because we don't know how to deal with
it all. It is too much. It is a heavy burden—more than
we can carry.

Then there are the small sufferings that become
a heavy burden. These sufferings can sometimes be
worse and have more power over us.

These are the small things that can just get to us and

bother us the whole day. They can occupy us—an ir-
ritating boss, traffic, an unfriendly gesture, a word of
rejection, mistakes at work. These are small things, but
they can take our joy away. The little things become
heavy burdens because they occupy us and take a place
in our heart.

Then we feel overburdened. We often say, "If I
just had that thing gone I'd be fine." But there is always just one thing. Everybody has some thorn in the
flesh. Everyone has something that makes them suffer
in some way. Though it may not be apparent at first,
every human heart carries a deep pain. Sometimes the
small crosses seem even harder to bear than the large
crosses. The church is supposed to be so full of love, but
sometimes in a church there are people who hate each
other. In your circle and community there is jealousy
and anger and it seems to be unbearable. Just where you
expect love there is conflict and pain.

And that is when we feel disconnected from God.
A burden becomes a heavy burden when it doesn't feel
connected to anything else. It is a burden that we have
to carry by ourselves and is not shared. It is not part of
anything larger. It just sits there and presses us down,
down, down.

Jesus says, "Take up your cross and follow me"
(Luke 9:23). He says, "Take up my burden. It is the
burden of the whole world and it will be a light burden.
Take up my yoke and it will prove to be an easy yoke"
(Matthew 11:30).

This is the mystery of the Christian life. It is not that God came to take our burden away or to take our cross away or to take our agony away. No. God came to invite us to connect our burden with God's burden, to connect our suffering with God's suffering, to connect our pain to God's pain.

The great invitation of the Christian life is to live a life of connectedness with the Son of God who died broken. It is an invitation to dare to live connected to God who wants to give us his burden as a light burden because it is a burden that God has already carried for us.

There is more. Not only is God compassionate with us, but we have to be willing to be compassionate with God. We have to *compati* with God. *Compati* is Latin for "suffer with"—we need to suffer with God.

The invitation to suffer with God is probably the most profound thing that we see in the Christian tradition. Compassion means not only that God suffers with us but that now we are invited to suffer with God.

St. Francis of Assisi, Teresa of Ávila, and John of the Cross speak about compassion. They speak about the mystery of suffering with Christ. They speak about their suffering as a participation in God's suffering, and by that connectedness their suffering loses its absurd quality. It is still painful. It is still hard. It is still agonizing. It is still difficult. It is still lonely. But connected with the cross it becomes something new.

Look at the man who is pierced and broken and you see the love of God radiating out to you. You feel the warmth and the newness streaming through you. Every time you look at your struggles, your pain, and your anguish as the burden you have to bear, see your struggles as being struggled with right there on the cross by the Son of God. Your struggle becomes a light burden because it is the burden of God and God has suffered for us.

To "take up the cross" does not mean to look for pain. It doesn't mean to go after the cross. It does not mean to search for a problem. We have a lot of problems. We don't need more. Sometimes we think that to "take up the cross" means to be hard on ourselves. That is not what Jesus says. To "take up the cross" means first of all to acknowledge where we are suffering, to recognize it.

Sometimes we focus on the big problems. I think we should start with focusing on our small problems.

We are suffering almost every moment of our life. There is always something that is a little hard. There is always some pain there that we sort of walk right over and don't take very seriously. But that pain is a cross. Are we taking it up? Are we acknowledging it? Are we saying yes? Often, it seems as if we are always willing to carry another type of cross than the one we already have.

"That person didn't speak to me today. It is not a big

deal but it hurts a little bit. This is a cross, a small one, but I acknowledge it as a cross."

"I didn't hear from my friend. That hurts a little bit. I don't need to walk right over these hurts as though they don't exist."

What is so remarkable is that just being able to see these little struggles allows us slowly to come home to our own house and not be so scared that something more fearful might come. We don't have to be afraid, because we are already able to acknowledge our struggle. We are familiar with it.

Jesus says, "Take up your cross." He didn't say, "Make up your cross," "Create your cross," or "Go after your cross." He said, "Take up your cross," and this means to have the courage to see your pain.

We live in a culture that constantly denies these interior pains. It doesn't hurt any less.

We say, "My friend died. I have to be strong."

It is very painful. There was a time when people mourned for a long time. They felt their pain and let the fruits of grief grow in them.

There are a lot of places where we are really in pain. Let us not ignore it. Let us not deny it but say, "Yes, this is difficult and I pick it up."

Acknowledge it. Say, "This is where I feel pain. It is my life and my life also means my pain. Can I stay with this? Can I recognize it and say yes? I can live this life. I want to live this life. It is painful and it has unique hurts but it is mine. I want to embrace it because I will never taste joy in life if I keep ignoring my pain."

It is the first thing that Jesus asks. He says, "Take up your cross. Take it up."

"Follow me." That is the second thing he asks.

Jesus says, "Make the carrying of your cross part of your discipleship. Connect it with me. Connect it with God's way."

We are called—we are urged—to bring our pain into the healing presence of the cross. That is what a life of prayer is all about. We pray when we say, "Lord, it hurts not to be liked by people that I love. I see how rejected you were and I want my experience of rejection to be connected with you."

Or we pray, "Lord, I am so fearful today. I don't know where it comes from, but I am anxious and fearful. It is there. Lord, I want to bring it into your presence and bring it right into the Garden of Gethsemane and connect it with your anguish so that my fear becomes your struggle. The struggle to live."

Somehow we have to have the courage to say, "My body aches, Lord. I am in physical pain. I don't know why the doctors can't help with the pain. But I want to know that you know what physical pain is too, and that you are a God who has a body that has risen, and in that body the wounds were visible. Wounds in your hands. Wounds in your feet. Wounds in your side. Let my woundedness become part of your woundedness so that my woundedness does not make me bitter or resentful, angry or upset, but brings me in touch with the mystery of your death and resurrection. I bring into your presence my whole being. I bring to you all my anguish and pain. Let my cross merge with yours. My burden becomes your burden and the experience fills me with new life and new hope."

That is what prayer is.

I worry a lot. You worry a lot. There are a lot of things we agonize over. We worry about tomorrow and yesterday, this person and that person. But are we really connecting it all? Are we bringing it into the present?

Bring it to the One who has already suffered through it all and has lifted it up in his Risen body.

Are you really making that connection so that something new can happen?

If that connection is being made, something new is being born. Every time a connection is made between us and the light of God, something new happens, some kind of renewal takes place in us. Every time we keep our pain isolated or hidden—"I am too embarrassed about it," "I can't tell anyone, it is too silly"—the burden becomes bigger and heavier.

When we pray, we connect our whole life with God's life. God's love can flow through our veins—our spiritual veins—through our heart and our being. We will discover a whole new way of being. We can live our struggles in a completely new way. All distinctions we make about our well-being—"I am happy," "I am sad"—can in some way be transcended into something very new.

Take your worries and convert them into prayer. Take your fear and connect it with God's fear. Take your depression and see it in the presence of God's dying on the cross. Bring it to the Presence who has suffered all and lived it all. You will discover that in the presence of Jesus you can live beyond pain and joy, sadness and gladness. When you pray, you connect your life with God's life. You live in a new way.

One time I was extremely depressed. I felt very sad about everything. I was in Flagstaff, Arizona, so I decided to go to the Grand Canyon. I saw billions of years of creation and realized that if those years represented an hour, I had been born not in the last second but in a tiny fraction of the last second.

Looking out, I thought, "My dear. Why all these problems?" Looking at the Grand Canyon, at that enormous abyss of beauty, the strange depression fell away. I felt the silence. In the face of this natural wonder, I thought, "What are you worrying about? As if you are carrying the burden of the world—a world that survived before you, and is something that will go on a long time after you. Why don't you just enjoy your life and really live it?"

This image of the Grand Canyon stayed with me for a long time. God is like the Grand Canyon. God suffered the wound, the wound of all humanity, and if I enter into the presence of that wound, my wound becomes a light burden or a light pain. Not because it is not there but because it has been embraced by love. I can live my pain and not be destroyed by it. I can acknowledge my pain and not be paralyzed by it. The Grand Canyon invited me to enter an abyss of divine love and to experience that I am immensely loved and cared for. I was invited to enter life with a new heart, with God's heart.

MANY OF US, if we are following Jesus at all, follow out of fear. But if we follow out of fear—fear of hell, of purgatory, of rejection, of not being acceptable—that is not following. Following Jesus cannot be a form of discipleship if it is out of fear. There is a lot of fear in us. Sometimes it overwhelms me how fearful we truly are.

We ask, "What happens if I don't follow him?"

"What will happen when I finally go up there? What am I going to say?"

Maybe we don't admit it, but sometimes we say, "Well, following Jesus is the safe way to go; you never know what is going to happen."

Jesus does not want us to follow him out of fear. He wants us to follow him out of love. Throughout the New Testament we hear, "Don't be afraid." An angel says it to Zechariah (Luke 1:13). An angel says it to Mary

(Luke 1:30). The angels at the tomb of the resurrection of Jesus say, "Do not be afraid" (Matthew 28:5). Jesus himself says, "Do not be afraid, it is I. Where I am you should not be afraid" (Matthew 14:27).

Fear is not of God, because God is the God of first love. As John says so beautifully, "First love casts out all fear" (1 John 4:18). The love of God is the perfect love that breaks through the boundaries of our fear. Jesus says, "Don't be afraid. Keep your eyes focused on me. Follow me."

Remember that last beautiful scene in the Gospel of John where Jesus says to Peter, "Simon, do you love me?" and Peter says, "Lord, you know I love you." Jesus asks a second time, "Simon, do you love me?" and Peter says, "You know I do." Jesus asks a third time, and Peter becomes rather disturbed. "Lord, you know I love you." "Okay, disciple," Jesus says, "feed my lambs, feed my sheep" (John 21:15–17). Then Jesus says the most important thing for us to hear right now. He says, "When you were young you girded yourself and you went where you wanted to go and when you are old you will stretch out your hands and someone else will gird you and lead you where you would rather not go" (John 21:18).

Jesus means, "When you are in love, when you are really in love, you can be guided to places that you have not chosen yourself. The person who loves can go to places where she or he would rather not go."

Jesus turns all psychology upside down.

He doesn't say, "When you are young you stretch out your hands and let other people gird you and when you grow old then you can do your own thing." No. Jesus says it the other way. He says, "When you are young you can do what you want to do and when you are old you will be led where you'd rather not go."

The spiritual life is a life in which we are more and more able to be led, to be guided to hard places, to places we would rather not go. For Jesus it was the cross. For Peter it was the cross. For Paul and all the disciples, it meant a lot of suffering. It is not masochism. It is not self-flagellation. It is not being hard on ourselves. It is being in love. It is being so fully and so totally in love that we go to places we would rather not go.

The interesting thing is that when we are in love we don't feel the pain in the way that other people think we would. If we are truly in love, our eyes are not focused on what hurts. Our eyes are focused on the person we love. We make one step, and another step, and another step, and another step. A mother or a father says, "Of course I will stay with my child who is sick. I love my child. I am not going to leave my child alone." Other people might say, "They are really suffering." But they have the energy to stay with their child who is ill, because they love their child so much.

When we are in love we can go to very difficult places and feel, not the pain first of all, but the love.

I am not saying that there is no suffering. I am only saying that our attention is not focused on it. Other people might say, "Oh, my dear, what suffering. What agony. How could anyone do all of that? It is terrible. I wouldn't be able to do it." From the outside their ability to live the suffering might look like an impossible feat.

When we go to work with the poorest of the poor or with people who are dying or in misery, or we give up a job to do other critical things, people might say, "My God, I don't know how you do it." Many of us can reply, "I am alive. It is easy. I don't see all those problems that you are speaking of. I am just following. I am guided to all these places that never in my life would I have thought I would go to."

A mother might have a child who is so sick that she has to stay with her for her whole life. She thought she could never handle losing her freedom in this way. Everyone asks her how she can do it. She says, "I can do it. I am not scared. I am in love. I am following."

Following the One with whom we are in love is the full meaning of following Jesus. We follow not out of fear but out of love.

❧

Dear Lord,

Give me eyes to see and ears to hear. I know there is light in the darkness that makes everything new. I know there is new life

in suffering that opens a new earth for me.
I know there is a joy beyond sorrow that
rejuvenates my heart. Yes, Lord, I know that
you are, that you act, that you love, that you
indeed are Light, Life, and Truth.

People, work, plans, projects, ideas,
meetings, buildings, paintings, music, and
literature can only give me real joy and peace
when I can see and hear them as reflections of
your presence, your glory, your kingdom.

Let me then see and hear. Lord, show me
your vision, become a guide in life and impart
meaning to all my concerns.

AMEN

(*from* The Only Necessary Thing)

CHAPTER FIVE

THE REWARD

"My Joy Will Be Yours"

Jesus says, "Very truly, I tell you, you will weep and mourn, but the world will rejoice; you will have pain, but your pain will turn into joy. When a woman is in labor, she has pain, because her hour has come. But when her child is born, she no longer remembers the anguish because of the joy of having brought a human being into the world. So you have pain now; but I will see you again, and your hearts will rejoice, and no one will take your joy from you."

JOHN 16:20–22

Then Jesus says, "I have said these things to you so that my joy may be in you, and that your joy may be complete."

JOHN 15:11

The reward of following Jesus is joy. It is part of being in love. We have to claim joy because that is the great gift Jesus came to bring us.

Joy is not an easy subject to articulate. We seem to be a lot better at talking about sorrow. But we have to learn to speak about joy, because joy is the great reward for those who take up the cross and follow Jesus.

Joy is hard to talk about but it is important to speak about because if you look around at people in most towns and cities you notice that people are so very serious. Very, very serious. It is amazing. If you walk down the street, people have serious faces. Everyone is doing very serious things. They are doing it and they are doing their thing and it has to be done now because it is urgent. It has to be done this week because it is very serious. The interesting thing is, that seriousness, that certainty, that certain somberness is quite often characteristic of people who are rather well off. When I am teaching at the divinity school it is hard to get a little smile out of anybody.

"Don't interrupt me. I have a paper to write. I have to be critical. And it is very important."

It seems that seriousness has something to do with accomplishment. We are involved in these projects. We have objectives and they have to be done. They have to be accomplished. And we are very, very serious about it.

Once, I lived in Lima, Peru, in an extremely poor

area. One thing that makes an overwhelming impression on anyone who visits—and I am not romanticizing—is that poor people, people with all kinds of difficulties, are not going to sit there and talk about those difficulties. Here's a little story:

I went to Lima because I thought it was a good idea to go there and do a project. I planned to do something about all that poverty. I was living with a family in a barrio outside the city limits called Pamplona Alta. It was a very dry type of desert land but with thousands of shacks built into the slopes of the surrounding hills. Every day I had to walk at least twenty minutes to get from the house where I was staying to the church. It was an incredible experience, because as I walked out of the house where I was living with Pablito, Maria, Sophia, Pablo, and little Johnny, little kids ran out of their houses to see me. They'd say, "Padrecito. Padrecito." They came from the houses and they grabbed me. They hadn't seen such a nice, tall American for a long time, and they reached out to me and before I knew it I had one kid on every finger! They didn't let me go.

"Let me go. I am going to help the poor!"

They really wouldn't let me go. They pulled me to the ground and I was sitting there in the sand with all these kids looking at me, touching me, feeling my legs. One kid looked in my mouth and said, "What a big mouth you have!" They were so excited just being with me, and there I was with my big five-year plan.

"I have to go. I am going to help the poor."

They were holding me and saying, "Play with us. Don't you see this is a nice day?"

These little children were telling me that if there is anything worth doing it is right in front of me. Here and now.

"Let's play ball. Let's just smile. Let's just laugh."

They were laughing, screaming, climbing, and making fun. It was just amazing. They could really celebrate!

The children made me realize that we have to get involved in a reverse mission, a mission from those who suffer in Latin America to us here in North America, so they can show us how suffering and agony are never totally without joy. Laughter and play are Divine healing.

I am not saying that oppression, hunger, and poverty should not be alleviated, but if we are not able to share in children's joy in the midst of their poverty, what do we really have to give?

Let's not be so serious as though we are the only ones able to save the world. Only God saves the world. That is something to stay joyful about.

It is hard to talk about joy. I had a professor in Holland who spent three years talking about anxiety. We studied Kierkegaard, Sartre, and Camus, and a lot of other people who made a career out of writing about anxiety. I asked him, "Can you do a lecture on joy?" He said, "I tried, but I don't have much to say about it."

When my leg hurts I can talk about it. I have a lot of words to describe how much it hurts. When it doesn't hurt I don't think about it. When I am well I don't talk about it. My language is limited. My language is much more elaborate for anxiety than for joy. Maybe this says something good about joy. Maybe we experience joy more often than we think. Maybe joyful living is what we are about. Maybe it is so normal that we don't need to talk about it.

The word I am going to use to talk about joy is ecstasy. It was given to me by Jean Vanier. Jean Vanier is a Canadian who created a worldwide community for and with people with intellectual disabilities. He said that after working with people with disabilities he thought that they of all people had a right to ecstasy. He told me that all people with disabilities should live ecstatic lives.

I started thinking about it, and realized that the word "ecstasy" means to move out ("ec") of the "static" place. Ecstasy means to move out of that which is static, that which is always the same. The ecstatic life is where we keep moving from a rigidly fixed situation to a new place. We are not content with the old. Joy is that ongoing movement out of the places of death, out of the places where things remain the same and are not moving. Everything in life changes. Where we see life we see change. And as soon as things stop changing, death appears. We become rigid, stiff, dead. It is very important for us to realize that joy is precisely that leaping toward life and moving away from the places that are the same. Joy is always about an experience of life as new.

Joy is connected to newness. No one ever says, "Oh, there is the old joy again." No! There is old sorrow, but there is no old joy. Joy is always new.

We say, "Wow! Isn't that exciting?" Newness always hits you as something beautiful, never seen before, something alive. For a little baby, every day is something new. It is never the old child again. It is always growing.

Joy is life because life means something is moving away from the old static places to new dynamic places.

The great challenge is to claim the joy that Jesus offers us. Jesus is God of the living. Jesus came to bring life, and life in abundance. Jesus came to break the chain of wounds and needs and to overcome death. He came to give life, and life is joy. "I want my joy to be yours and for your joy to be complete" (John 15:11). Jesus says, "I came to overcome death and to give you life that does not end."

It is not easy for us to live this way, because something in us is afraid. There is a resistance to joy. Something in us is tempted to choose death instead of life, to choose the fixed place instead of the place of joy. Fear does this to us. Fear makes us cling to the fixed place. Fear holds us to the ordinary, to the normal, to where we feel secure.

Two things can happen when we are afraid. One is that we stick to the familiar ways of doing things. The other is that we panic and run all over the place. The first is called routine behavior and the other is called rootless behavior. Both involve fear.

Routine Behavior

Think about it. When we get scared we choose familiar patterns, traditional ways. We say, "This is the way I do things here, so don't come up with new ideas." "There is nothing new under the sun." "Let's just leave things as I have done them." "You know, I have some experience and therefore I always do it the same way."

Fear makes people cling to security. Some of us prefer to be secure and a little miserable rather than insecure and vitalized. Some of us hold to our complaints like a security blanket. When asked, "How are you doing?" we respond, "Fine, but I still have my complaints. Don't think I am all that fine!" We get a strange kind of satisfaction from our complaints.

We talk about people negatively, or about ourselves negatively, or about our health or about whatever. We feel secure because we can hang around places and have something to talk about. We can sit around a table and complain and we feel a little bit safe in our complaints, our nice little gossiping, our nice little "Not good, never will be good, so let's sit around. This is how things are. Let's repeat it again."

We feel a kind of security in not wanting to move. "Let's just hold on to where we are. We won't be any better anyhow. Let's be realistic."

When we are afraid we keep choosing security. When we become aware of this, examples of choosing security start leaping out at us, not only individual choices for security but also choices made by the collective society to secure itself. We begin to realize that the concern of the world for security is connected with fear.

We build bombs to be secure. We defend ourselves from the enemy. We realize that security concerns make us all dead before the bombs have exploded. They make us stiff and rigid.

Just the fear of war does a lot of destruction—in our children, in our own mind, in our own hearts. It makes us fear for it. It makes us afraid to live and makes us perpetually concerned about our security. We use so much money, time, talent, and energy preparing for a war that might never happen. Nevertheless, it can destroy our minds and hearts and makes us hug the forces of death. This is dangerous.

And there is no joy there.

The more we make security our primary concern the harder it is to be joyful. To be joyful means to jump out of that place of safety and to try something new.

It is a constant discipline to keep moving away from the fearful places and to choose joy. We have to constantly choose between security and freedom, joy and life.

Rootless Behavior

There is another response to fear that is not about security or routine. It is precisely the opposite. It is rootlessness.

Fear not only makes us grab for the safe places, it also makes us just splash around. There are people who get so panicky and so afraid of doing routine things that they go all over the place. They lose their roots, they pull up their anchors. They are just wandering wild and they don't know what to do. It is like their fear has become so big that they don't know from one day to the next what they are doing.

They just sort of hang around in the world. They do a little bit here and a little bit there, and they kind of move from one little excitement to the other—sexual excitement, or drinking excitement, or drugs excitement, or a quick deal here or a quick deal there, but they are not feeling at home anywhere. They have lost their roots. They wander from here to there.

That is not joy. That is not freedom.

If we don't have an anchor, we run around anxiously, nervously doing things, but there is no place of home. If we don't have a sense of at-homeness there is no joy in moving.

Jesus speaks a lot about this. He says, "At the end of the world people are going to run around. There will be debauchery and drunkenness. But don't follow them. Don't lose your roots." "You," he says, "pray unceasingly and stand with your head erect in the presence of the Son of Man." Jesus says, "Have a sense of confidence. Remain rooted. Remain connected. Remain in love."

Fear makes us grab traditional, routine ways of doing things. Or it might be so intense that it throws us for a loop and makes us run around wild. Both types of behavior are not the Christian joy that Jesus speaks about.

Joy

What is joy? What is the real ecstasy?

Let's look at Jesus for a moment. I don't know if Jesus was ever funny. I don't think so. I am not even sure he was happy. But he was filled with joy. The joy of Jesus is a joy that is born out of his ongoing intimacy with God. Joy flows from that communion with the Father. Joy springs from Jesus' intimate belonging to the Father. Jesus says, "You might leave me. Everybody might forget about me. But the Father will never leave me. The Father is faithful. The Father is with me."

Try to hear what Jesus is talking about. Jesus is talking about a deep sense of belonging. A deep listening.

Obedience means listening with your whole body. *Ob-audire* in Latin means careful listening. Jesus is the obedient one. He is always listening to the Father. He is always connected to the source from where he comes. He never feels alone. Even when people betray him, even when people nail him to the cross, spit in his face, and flagellate him, he never loses the connection with God. Even when he doesn't feel it anymore he doesn't lose it. When he says, "My God, My God, why have you forsaken me?" he doesn't feel God's presence, but he knows. He says, "My Father never leaves me alone." It is there that the joy is anchored. It is anchored in that connection.

Jesus is able to move around in the most difficult situations, not only physically and emotionally, but spiritually. He can explore new ways of loving because he is rooted in God. He breaks right through routines when they become rigid and no longer serve God. He criticizes the Pharisees who were stuck in routines.

Jesus also warns people about living rootless lives. He says, "Remain in me as I remain in you. I love you with the same love that the Father loves me." He is speaking about the inner connectedness of life. Life-giving connectedness is what allows Jesus to move out of the places of death toward life. The experience of joy that Jesus offers is not happiness. It is not just feeling "up." Joy is something else. The joy of Jesus is never disconnected from sorrow.

The world is very strange. The world divides our

experience of sorrow and joy into two separate emotional states: sadness and happiness. It says, "The world is very sorrowful so we need to have happy moments in between to survive." Like happy hour. "Let's create a bit of happiness to forget our sorrow." The world says, "Life is basically sad, depressing, and sorrowful, but let's create little islands of happiness." A lot of commercial products are connected to this. Companies create little toys to make you feel happy for a little moment. But momentary happiness is not what Jesus means when he speaks about joy.

Joy is also not some kind of happy medium between rootlessness and routine. It is not that. Joy is not a momentary vacation from the heaviness of life. Joy is not something to escape the problems of the world. The joy that Jesus offers is of a spiritual order. It is not just an emotional thing. It is not just a physical thing. It is a spiritual gift. The gift of joy.

Joy is a gift that is there even when we are sorrowful, even when we are in pain, even when things are difficult in our lives. The joy that Jesus offers is a joy that exists in very, very difficult situations. I've met people who, when I look objectively at their life, make me think, "My good person, how can you live with all this sorrow, all this anguish?" Yet still, there is all this joy there that doesn't depend on how things are going day after day. There is something deeper. There is a deep connectedness.

What we have to start sensing is that in the spiritual life, joy is embracing sorrow and happiness, pain and pleasure. It is deeper, fuller. It is more. It is something that remains with us. It is something of God that is very profound. It is something we can experience even when we are in touch with very painful things in our lives. If there is anything the church wants to teach us it is that the joy of God can be with us always—in moments of sickness, in moments of health, in moments of success, in moments of failure, in moments of birth, in moments of death. The joy of God is never going to leave us.

We can get a glimpse of it. For instance, if we talk to people who work with the dying, we realize that those people can be very joyful. People who work in hospices and people working in nursing homes face death every day, yet while they are always involved in so-called "sad" situations they are often joyful people. We realize that the joy they have in their hearts is of another nature than just success or failure, birth or death. Sometimes we see people working with the poorest of the poor and when they come to the United States or to a place where there is wealth, they can't wait to go back to their people again. Why is that? They don't like misery. They are people who have learned to live with joy that is not taken away from them when they live with the poor. In fact, the suffering brings them in touch with their own joy, which is deeper than the material things we often use as a substitute for true happiness.

We have to realize that in the spiritual life there is something very different going on from what the world teaches us. We are surrounded by voices telling us that we have to have worldly success, but Jesus is saying, "Go with me to where the poor are, to where the broken are, and there you will find joy. Happy are the poor, happy are the mourning, happy are those who are persecuted. Joyful are the poor, those who are making peace, and those who are persecuted." The whole thing is upside down, because in the eyes of God the joy is hidden right in the center of the sorrow.

Joy is hidden right in the heart of human pain. We can dare to look up at Jesus on the cross, see his execution, and say, "In the cross there is my joy." We can speak about the cross as a sign of hope because we know that the closer we come to the cross, the closer we come to new life. Somehow the sorrow that we experience is like birth pain. We feel like new life is going to burst out. The agony, pain, and suffering of your life and mine are experienced as ways to give birth to something completely new.

It is precisely by entering more fully and deeply into the reality of our painful existence that we can touch the joy that wants to leap up in us as the child in the womb of Elizabeth leaps up in joy. It doesn't mean that Elizabeth didn't have sorrow. It is that she knew that joy was born out of her sorrow. The mystery of life is that Jesus came to suffer with us so that we could be joyful. He didn't come so we wouldn't suffer but so that we could taste that eternal life, that lasting joy that is of God, that is already in this world, already now, already precisely here.

When we can face our own painful situation, we will discover that hidden in the pain is the treasure—a joy that is there for us to experience here and now.

It is very important that we get in touch with this. That is what the spiritual life—the life with God—is about. It is being in touch with that love that becomes joy in us. Once we know that place in us, we come in touch with that solid undercurrent that flows underneath all our ups and downs. Underneath all our fluctuations is a deep solid divine stream that is called joy. The love of God that touches us and informs us is a love that we can trust is there. No one can take it away from us. All the great saints talk about it. All people who have suffered talk about it. It is the place that is home. The place of God. The place where you are safe. The place where the world has no power over you. Jesus says, "You do not belong to the world. You belong to God. To me. To the Father. To the Spirit. You are called to live in the world without being of it."

How Can We Be Joyful? How Can We Bring Joy into Our Lives?

There is one word that is very important to talk about. The word is "celebration."

Celebration is, first of all, living out of joy. Celebration is what we are called to. We are called to practice joy by celebrating.

We have to learn how to celebrate life. Celebrating life is not a party, but an ongoing awareness that every moment is special and asks to be lifted up and recognized as a blessing from on high. When I was with Jean Vanier and the people with intellectual disabilities, I saw them doing this all the time. The church invites us to celebrate. Christmas, Epiphany, Easter, Lent, Pentecost—we celebrate the holy year. We celebrate birthdays and anniversaries, we celebrate Thanksgiving, we celebrate memorial days. We celebrate.

But that is only part of celebrating. We have to go further. To celebrate means to lift up the moment and say, "This is God's moment." To celebrate is to lift up today and say, "This is the day the Lord has made." And not just on Thanksgiving but also on Monday morning. Let us be glad and joyful. Let us celebrate! If we are able to celebrate life, and not only on special occasions, we realize that we have many occasions to be glad. We realize that something is happening, that something is coming through, and we have to rejoice.

Let me tell you another story:

As I mentioned earlier, when I was in Peru the people I was staying with were very poor. They didn't have anything. I slept on the roof because they didn't have a room for me. They just put a bed up there. It never rains in Peru. There are always clouds, but it never rains. After several months of living there, I said to them, "I am going to leave next week." They couldn't have cared less because since I was still there I wasn't leaving. It didn't register. But finally on Saturday morning, I said, "I am leaving in an hour." I had my suitcase and they saw that I was leaving. Because they loved me and I loved them, Sophia, the mother, gave little Johnny some money and he ran out to the store. It was noon and my bus was leaving in thirty minutes and I started to get nervous. But little Johnny came back and he had a big bottle of Coke and two cookies. He said, "We'll have a party." He filled the family's one glass and took the glass to each person for a little sip. Then he broke the cookies into little pieces and shared them with everyone. Pablito, the boy of thirteen, said, "Let's have a bit of music." There was this old, cranky record player, I don't know where it came from, but he said, "Let's have some music," and he made it go. He said, "Let's dance!" It was twelve noon. I have to leave at 12:15 and we're having this party. A little Coca-Cola, a little bit of cookie, and a little dancing. They were laughing and laughing and saying goodbye. Then they took my suitcase and everyone walked me to the bus. There was a big farewell and I realized that we had just celebrated the Eucharist.

What a gift those people had to bring me in touch with joy. I was in touch with their poverty, their issues, their medical care. It was all very real and they needed a lot of help, but in the midst of it they remained joyful.

Celebration doesn't mean to celebrate only the good moments. Ecstatic joy embraces all of life and does not shy away from painful moments, departures, and even death. Death is celebrated not because it is desirable but because death has no final power over us. There is never a death that cannot bear fruit.

We can celebrate pain not because pain is good but because we can pray with it and break bread together. Difficult moments can be lifted up. We lift them up in gratitude.

Celebration is really an expression of gratitude. Death doesn't have the final word. Even agony, pain, struggles, war, all of that, is somehow not the final power. God is a God of the living.

"You shall have life and life abundantly."

For people with disabilities, life can be hard. Yet Jean Vanier and the people with disabilities always have something to celebrate. Their homes are filled with little candles, decorations, flowers, and song. There is never a day that isn't lifted up in gratitude to the Giver of Life.

The more we celebrate, the more we realize that we are in communion. To celebrate is to create community. It is the first sign of the Kingdom proclaimed among us. Celebration is the way in which faith in the God of Life is lived out, whether there are smiles or tears. Celebration reveals the deep undercurrent of joy that flows beneath all of our ups and downs.

Jesus rewards us with joy. Not only later, but now. Not only in the happy moments but also in our sorrow. Joy is hidden in our suffering and revealed in our communal life.

THERE IS ANOTHER aspect of following Jesus that might be a little hard to understand right away. Following Jesus does not just mean following Jesus who lived two thousand years ago. Some of us say, "I wish I could have lived then. It is too bad that it was two thousand years ago and I have to imagine Jesus. I have to fantasize about this man who lived so long ago, whom I never met. I will use my memory to follow this man, this Jesus of Nazareth. I will try to do what he told us to do then and apply it to our times now."

But following Jesus means much more than following a memory of someone. It is more than following someone we imagine, someone we dream about, someone we try to evoke with our imagination. Following Jesus means following the Risen Lord. Following Jesus means following the Lord who is the Lord of history, the Lord who is with us now and here, at this moment. It is not a sentimental memory. It is not a pious feeling about someone we hardly know. No. It is being guided by the One who is with us here and now. It is being led by the One who is really present among us as the Lord, who rose from the dead and became the Lord who embraces all people, in all times, and is therefore the Lord of the now, the present, the here.

It is very important to understand this distinction.

In my house I have an icon by Andrei Rublev that I found in Jerusalem. It is an icon of the Risen Lord. It is not just Jesus of Nazareth. It is the Risen Lord. The Lord who became flesh. The Lord who lived among us in Nazareth, in Bethlehem, and in Jerusalem but was raised up and was given a name, which is above all other names, so that in that name every knee would bow and would praise him as Lord.

This icon has become the centerpiece of my little chapel at home. I want you to realize that the One you and I are called to follow is the Lord of history, the Risen Lord who is the Gate to Heaven, the Door to Eternal Life, who is the Way, the Truth, and the Life, who is the only Son of God, full of majesty and glory, who is the Giver of abundant life, who is our Lord, always drawing us closer into the mystery of God's life. He is not a cozy friend whom you have a chat with. That is not the spiritual life. He is the Lord who calls you into communion with God.

If you look at the eyes of this icon, they are quite stern. But beyond those eyes lies the eternity of God's love. It is not a Jesus that you walk around with to get where you are going. It is someone who leads you into the life eternal. By praying to the Lord of history, and by following the Lord of history, you will be drawn into that mystery of God's eternal love. You will discover that if you pray with this icon, with this image, you will find that this is the Lord who is stern because he is the judge but also gentle because he is the compassionate Lord. He is the Lord who is full of love and calls you to that love. He is the Lord of truth and of beauty. You will discover that following Jesus is following the Lord who speaks to you day after day and calls you always to a deeper and deeper communion with God.

Following Jesus is entering more and more into the intimate mystery of God. God became flesh so that we could be led through him, with him, and in him in the glory of God the Father in communion with the Spirit. The icon of the Risen Lord is a reminder of the great vocation that we all have—the vocation to grow closer to that great mystery.

Lord Jesus,

In the middle of busy work and many concerns
I want to fix my eyes on you. You are the
Lord, the Lord who calls me to your kingdom,

the Lord who calls me to find rest with you, the Lord who calls me to conversion, to new life, to new hope. I am grateful, O Lord, that you call me here. Help me to be renewed so that through me many can be healed and find new life.

AMEN

✳

THE PROMISE
"I Will Be with You Always"

Jesus said to his disciples, "I must tell you the truth. It is for your own good that I am going, because unless I go the Advocate will not come to you. But if I do go I will send him to you. I shall ask the Father and he will give you the Spirit to be with you forever. The Spirit of Truth, whom the world can never receive since it neither sees nor knows him. But you know him because he is with you. He is in you."

JOHN 16:7–15

He said to them, "All authority in heaven and on earth has been given to me. Go therefore, make disciples of all the nations; baptize them in the name of the Father and of the Son and of the Holy Spirit, and teach them to observe all the commands I gave you. And know that

I am with you always, yes, to the end of the time."

The first time that the Lord God reveals God's name is when God speaks to Moses in the burning bush. God says, "My name is I AM. The God of Abraham, Isaac, and Jacob" (Exodus 3:6). That means that when God reveals himself to his people, he reveals himself as the God with his people, because "I AM" literally means "I am the one who is with you." It means "I AM the faithful God, the God who journeys with you," "I am the God who comes to be with you and remain with you. I AM. I AM myself faithful to you."

The words "I AM" mean "the one who stays with you," "the one who will not leave you alone," "the one who will journey with you through the desert and help you find a new life." God says, "I AM your companion, your fellow traveler, the God who loves you so much that I will be with you always. I will be a torch in the night so that you can find your way. I will be a cloud during the day so that you can travel to the promised land. I am your God who will never leave you alone, who will be with you so that you can find your way."

One of the most beautiful aspects of the Christian faith is that when Jesus appears, he appears as Emmanuel, as God-with-us. In Jesus, we realize how serious God is about his promise to be with us and to stay with us. In Jesus, the faithfulness of God becomes even more visible because in Jesus, God became flesh and dwelled among us. He pitched his tent among us. He lived among us. He did not want to keep any distance from us. He wanted to be one of us.

God-with-us. Emmanuel.

Jesus, therefore, reveals God as a God who wants to be even closer to his people than his people could ever possibly imagine. The great good news of the Gospel is precisely that God wants to be with us to share our struggle, walk our way, suffer our pain, and die our death, so that we are able to say, "There is nothing human that God does not share with us." That is the great good news. God is with us in every aspect of our lives.

There is one more mystery that we seldom fully grasp or even think about: Jesus is not the last word. There is something more. There is something that is an even greater way of being with us. Jesus says to us, "It is good for you that I leave, because when I leave I can send my Spirit and my Spirit will be able to dwell in you" (John 16:7). Here Jesus reveals to us that God wants to be with us in a way that is so intimate and so personal that we can say that God dwells in us, that God is most intimately in us. God-with-us is the God who travels with us in the Old Testament and the One who suffers with us. And God is also God-in-our-breath. We breathe the Spirit of God.

What more intimate communion can you imagine

than the breath? It is so intimate, so deep, that you don't even reflect on it. You don't say, "I am breathing well today." You never say that, because it is so intimate, because your breathing is you. And it is that closeness that God chose so that God could become our breath. "Spirit," *pneuma*, means breathing.

Jesus says, "It is good for you that I go, so that I can send you my breath, so that you can breathe my life in you." We start seeing what it means when Jesus finally says, "I will be with you always until the end of time." He means, "I will be so intimately with you that you and I are one. You can breathe my breath and you can say, 'Not I live anymore, but Christ lives in me.'"

You and I are called to become other Christs, to be living manifestations of God in this world. God dwells in us in such an intimate way that we indeed are becoming manifestations of God's glory in this world. That is the great mystery. That is the great promise. That is the promise of the Spirit.

How Do We Respond to the Promise?

When Jesus says, "I will be with you always," we have to reflect what this presence really means and how it affects us. I want to say three things about it. First of all, I want to speak about the presence of God in absence. Second, I want to speak about the presence of God that creates in us a desire for the future and moves us forward. Finally, I want to speak about a presence that we can practice concretely in our daily life.

Presence revealed through absence

Sometimes a person can grow closer to us not only in her or his presence but also in her or his absence. We grow closer to one another not just by presence but also by absence, not only by coming but also by leaving. We grow more intimate by a constant leaving and returning.

I want us to feel that for a moment, because that is how we might come in touch with the mystery of the spiritual life.

Let me give you a few examples.

When you leave your father and your mother, it is only after you have left your home, your family, that you can see your parents in a new way and experience a new intimacy with them.

I experienced this in my own life. I grew up in Holland, and when I moved to the United States I had to leave my parents, but that absence made me come in touch with them in a new way. We felt a new intimacy, a new communion. It was as if I couldn't see them when I was with them but needed some distance to recognize how much they loved me. Only by being away from them was I able to see their love clearly and profoundly.

When I was home with them in the kitchen or the living room, it all seemed so ordinary, but when I took a step away, I saw something and felt something I hadn't seen or felt before I left. My relationship with them deepened through absence.

Let me give you another example.

We visit somebody and we might have a rather normal conversation with the person, but what is so interesting is that often the memory of that visit is as powerful as the visit itself. The person who was sick might say, "I was sick and he came and visited me." In the absence of the person who came to visit us, a gratitude, a love, can grow that wasn't experienced in his or her presence. That is why it is important that we visit one another. Not because so much is happening in the visit but because the leaving might be as important as the being together. When we visit a sick friend we can say, "I can only be with you for an hour or two. I have other things to do. But it is good for you that I leave, because when I leave you might start thinking about this visit as something good for you. I might leave some of my spirit behind with you so that you know that while I am leaving I am also sending something new." Many of us have had this experience. When a person leaves us we realize how much we are loved by that person. We might not be able to express that in his or her presence, but we can experience it. We can feel that in his or her absence.

Or take another example: letter writing.

Don't you think that in written words we can say things that we could never say face-to-face? We need a little absence to reflect on the person, and then we can sit down and write, "I love you. You mean a lot to me. I care a lot for you." We wouldn't be able to say it in the presence of that person because it sounds a little embarrassing, a little difficult, a little too direct. But when we have taken a little distance we can write, "I am thinking about you. I am so grateful that I know you. I want you to know that I care for you." We realize that while we write the letter an intimacy grows in us. The person who is absent grows more intimately in our heart and we feel in communion with that person as though that person's spirit lives in us. There is a new intimacy there that is only possible in absence, with distance. It creates a desire to see that person again. Without absence the desire might not be that strong.

Perhaps the most profound example of presence in absence is our death and the death of those we love. I believe we can grow in love with people who have left us through death. We only know each other partially in life but as people of faith we come to know each other in a new way through death.

Somehow we have to dare to say, "Brother, sister, it is good for you that I leave, that I die, because when I am dead you will discover me in a new way. When I die I will become present to you in a new way." I am sure many of you have lost parents, children, or friends. Some of you might recognize that a new intimacy can grow in you with those who have died. Their memory becomes a real, active presence in your life.

We might discover that all those people who have died in our life have taken up a place in our heart and keep nurturing us. They keep leading us along, they keep deepening our lives. This is a great mystery. It is a mystery that Jesus reveals to us in the most fulsome way. He says, "It is good for you that I am going, because if I do not leave I cannot send my Spirit. When I leave, I will send you my Spirit and my Spirit will lead you to the full truth" (John 16:7).

The word "truth" doesn't mean doctrine or dogma, but a full "betrothal" relationship ("troth" means truth). "I give you intimacy. My Spirit will lead you to the full betrothal with God and only my leaving will make that possible." The death of Jesus is a death that is for our good, so that the Spirit of Jesus can lead us to that most intimate communion with God.

Jesus' leaving was good. He could not be understood in his lifetime. His disciples did not understand him. The disciples didn't know what Jesus was talking about. All the way to the end, to the death of Christ, they ran away. On the mount of ascension they still doubted it. They said, "Well, weren't you supposed to restore Israel to power?" "Weren't you supposed to throw the Romans out?" "Weren't you supposed to fix the political situation here?" They didn't know.

They didn't know when Jesus said, "This is my body. This is my blood." They didn't understand when he said, "I am the life. I am the resurrection. I am the Door. I am the Truth." They had inklings, but they kept translating it to fit their own limited perspectives.

But Jesus kept saying, "I am telling you now so that later you will understand. I tell you these things now because when I am gone you will know what I am talking about. You will know because I will send my Spirit and my Spirit will reveal to you everything I have taught you. All I learned from my Father, the Spirit will teach you."

It is so important for us to realize that Jesus had to leave for us to understand who Jesus truly was. The disciples were confused. But Jesus said, "Don't go out. Don't start doing things. Just wait until the Spirit comes."

When the Spirit did come, everything changed because they saw and they understood. They realized that they had been a part of something special. Suddenly they could start living an interior life, a life in Christ. They might have traveled with Christ, but before the Spirit came they could not travel in Christ. Before Jesus died they could not say, "Not I live, but Christ lives in me." They couldn't say that.

They could say that only when the Spirit had come and the breath of Christ, the Spirit of Christ, had come into them. They could say, "I am the living Christ." "Not I live, but Christ lives in me." They became other Christs, they became living presences of God.

As soon as they discovered they had the life of

Christ within them all boundaries broke open and they went all over the world. The great mystery of the Holy Spirit is that Christ is Christ-with-us through the ages. Christ is Christ-within-us in the most intimate way. We can say that it is God-with-us but also Christ-with-us who sends us out to the whole world and to all the countries, nations, and peoples.

We don't have to be limited to one country or another, because in Christ-in-the-Spirit all places are ours. All the world is ours to travel, because we are already home. We are already in God. We have already found a communion and we don't have to limit that to any family, any country, or any circumstance.

I hope this starts to make sense to you. It is hard to say it well. It is the great mystery. We can live a spiritual life, a life in which the Spirit of Christ dwells in us. We can live a life in which the Spirit sets us free of limitations. The Spirit frees us to be home wherever we are sent.

And this happens in absence, in the absence of Jesus, who says, "I send you out until I come again."

Presence revealing the future

"The Spirit will tell you of the things to come."

For us the future is often a source of anxiety and fear. We have all kinds of questions: What if my children get sick, I lose my job, my wife or husband leaves me, or a war breaks out? Our fears pull us away from the present and extinguish the Spirit in us.

When we believe that God is with us always through the Spirit, we can let the future emerge out of the present. When we really believe that God is with us and that we are already now breathing his Spirit, we don't have to worry about the future. We don't have to worry about what might happen next. We can start trusting that if we fully live the life in the Spirit, the future will unfold from the present as we travel through life.

One of the greatest temptations of our lives is to live ahead of ourselves and not believe that something is happening here and now. The world in which we live makes us believe that the real thing is happening next week, next month, or next year. As Christians, we are challenged to believe that what is happening is always happening here and now. At this moment. Now. If we live the now, the present, to the full, the future will grow. It will reveal itself to us because we have already received the Spirit. We have already received the beginning of the eternal life. We are already in the House of God. We are already breathing God's breath. Let's stay there and listen carefully.

There is this wonderful word in the Gospel and it is "patience." In the Gospel to have patience means to stay fully where you are, to live the moment to the full, to trust that all that you need is where you are. An impatient person is always saying, "This is not a good place to be. I want to be somewhere else." "This moment is empty." "This moment doesn't hold anything for me. I want to be there." "Tomorrow, next year, later, when I grow old, when I get a career, when I get rich," or whatever.

We are always looking ahead. We are in grade school to go to high school. We are in high school to go to college. We are in college to get our little job. We are in our little job to get our big job. We are in our big job to retire. We retire . . . but the real thing is always ahead of us. A lot of us live ahead of ourselves and therefore are not tasting the truth that the Spirit of God is with us now, here, at this moment.

Jesus says, "Be patient." Patience means to remain close to the moment and to fully taste where you are so that the seeds that are sown in the moment can grow and lead you to the future. The future is hidden in the present as a seed in fertile ground. By nurturing and tending the soil in which we stand we come in touch with the promise.

Don't be impatient. Don't go back and pull out the seed to see if it is growing. It will not grow if you do that. Trust that a promise is given to you and that it is hidden in the soil on which you stand. It will grow into a strong tree but you have to give it time. It will reveal the future to you and it will grow right where you are. Trust that that is what the Spirit does.

The good news is that our present moment is not

empty but full. In the fullness of time God came to us. Our time has become full time because the Spirit has been sent to us, because the Lord is with us, and this is all that we ever wanted—to live with the Lord, to live with God. If that is our deepest desire why then, when God sends us his Spirit, and sends us his breath, isn't that enough? I ask you now, can you be fully present to the moment where you are breathing?

We have to learn to live fully in the present, because God is always the God of now, of here. The day in which we live is the day of the Lord. If anything is happening that is spiritually valid, it is happening here and now, at this moment. As you sit here. As you pray. It is always here. The great art of spiritual living is to pay attention to the breathing of the Spirit right where you are and to trust that there will be breathing of new life. The Spirit will reveal itself to you as you move on. That is the beauty of the spiritual life. You can be where you are. You don't have to be anywhere else. You can be fully present to the moment and trust that even in the midst of your pain, in the midst of your struggle, something of God is at work in you and wants to reveal itself to you.

Be here.

Be quiet.

Listen.

Practicing Presence

How do we practice the presence of God? Through prayer and service.

Prayer

Prayer is entering into the presence of God here and now. Prayer is the way in which we become present to the moment and listen to God who is with us. God is always where we are. God is with us until the end of time. We have to be here. We have to listen. We have to be attentive. Prayer is the discipline of attentiveness, of being here.

I really want to ask you to practice prayer as a practice of the presence of God. You don't have to say many words. You don't have to have deep thoughts. You don't have to worry about how to think. You can just be where you are and say, "I love you. I love you. I know you love me and I love you. I don't have any big things to say. I don't have any profound words to express, but I am here and I want you to be with me and I want to be with you." It is that simple. It is a very simple thing. Prayer is not complicated. It is not difficult. If people ask you how you pray just tell them, "Sit down and say, 'Lord, here I am.' "

Distractions mean that we are being pulled into the past or into the future. That is what a distraction is.

We start thinking about what happened yesterday or what is happening tomorrow. Distractions mean we are not yet fully here. We are not fully present yet. That is okay. You have to smile to yourself and say, "I am distracted. I am not fully here. I am not fully trusting. I am still all over the place. I want to pray, but I am still thinking about this person who got to me yesterday and I wish I could give her a little talk," or "Tomorrow, I have to go to work and my son has to go to the hospital, and I have to see this person tomorrow to discuss a promotion." Sure, that is us—we are never totally here. If we were totally here we would be in heaven so we are never totally here. We are a little bit in the past, a little bit in the future, and all over the place, actually.

But even so, it is very important to say, "I want to be more here because I know that you, God, are here. I know you love me. I know that all I need is here and therefore I am going to sit here for a moment and say thank you for being a faithful God, thank you for your name I AM. Thank you for your Son, Jesus, who came to be with us. Thank you for the Spirit, who dwells in me so deeply that I don't even feel it all the time or experience it, but I know it. I know, just as I know that I am breathing without feeling that breath all the time, so I know that you, God, are with me even if I don't feel it all the time."

Prayer is that simple presence that we have to practice. I promise you, if you practice prayer you will be fully rewarded. God does not wait long to tell you how close he is to you. A lot of struggles you have about the past or the future might become less painful or less dominating or less imprisoning. They will always be there—you will always be distracted and always be worrying—but you have a place in yourself that is rather free of it. You have your fears, your anxieties, and they are all around you, but in the center of all the storms there is this quiet place where you can say, "I love you. You love me. It is here and now. It is good to be here. It is good to be in your presence, Lord. I don't need anything else."

Service

Service is being involved in something that is for the people of God.

At times, we might be involved in larger things—clothing the naked, sheltering the poor, helping the refugees, visiting the sick or imprisoned, but it is always small to begin with. It begins with small gestures. Being kind to your family and the people you work with, saying a patient word, writing a card, sending a flower.

Be attentive. Be attentive. Be attentive.

When we pray frequently and know that God is in us here and now, we are very attentive to others because we are less preoccupied with ourselves. We are less worried about ourselves and if we are not very worried about ourselves we see other people more clearly. We see their struggle. We see their beauty. We see their kindness. We see that they are not trying to hurt us but that they have their own problems. We are much gentler, because we are in the presence of the Spirit. We realize these people are also struggling.

This is one of the greatest and first rewards of following Jesus. Suddenly, the Spirit in you sees the Spirit in them. The Christ in you sees the Christ in them. The heart of God in you sees the heart of God in them. Spirit speaks to Spirit, heart speaks to heart, and Christ speaks to Christ. You cannot see Christ in the world, but the Christ in you can see Christ in the world. You cannot see God in the world, but God in you can see God in the world. The spiritual life is the recognition of the Spirit, in the Spirit, for the Spirit. It is the mutuality of the Spirit seeing the Spirit. It is the mutuality of God praising God.

We begin to see how good people are underneath all their violence, their hatred, their revenge, their illusions, and their aspirations. We realize they are people of God and that the Spirit of God also blows through them and breathes in them. We realize that people are wonderful, that they are beautiful, that they are persons sounding through the love of God. We see it and are glad. We can say, "It is good to be with you, because you remind me even more of God's love." Community starts forming. New life starts taking place.

We do not do service to earn anything. It is not an

anxious need to save the world. We don't act on the condition that change will take place. No. You can see how intense that might become. If our only concern is "I better help him or her," or to do things to change a person or the world, or the country, or the politics, or the social condition—if change is the condition of service—we are going to be very bitter and very soon. But if service is an expression of gratitude for the love we have already experienced then we can be free and engage in change without trying so hard. Service is an expression of the gift you have within you that you want to share with others.

In a way, service is an act of gratitude. We are so full of God's presence, we are so aware of God's promise, that we don't want to hold it back. We want to share it. The disciples went around the world to announce that God is with us and that we can already now enjoy his presence. The disciples' concern for the poor, the hungry, the sick, and the dying was an expression of a deep faith in God's presence. "What you do for the least of mine, you do for me" (Matthew 25:40).

When you practice the presence of God, you will find yourself drawn to the poor, to people who are struggling, to places where people are in pain. You want other people to realize that God is with them. Service means to simply bear witness to that new life in you.

The Spirit in you will draw you closer to those who suffer or to those in pain, because you will see there the presence of God. We want to be there with the people and reveal to them that God has not left them alone. We want to tell the world that something great is happening and that the Spirit is not just for us but for them too. We want to call forth. We want to say, "Trust that the Spirit of God is within you and live according to that Spirit. It will make all things new.

"You will have more energy than you thought. You thought you were broken, and you are, but in the midst of your brokenness and poverty there is something in you. You have a gift. Let that gift come to fruition in you."

All the little actions that you do are actions of gratitude. Human service, action for your neighbor, whether it is small or large, whether it involves individuals, communities, or countries, actions of service are to be done out of gratitude.

They have to be acts of *eukharistia* (eucharist, gratitude).

Acts of service have to be an expression of the fact that God has come to us and dwells in us, and that God has already given us a life eternal because he has already given us his breath. We are already in God. We have already overcome in principle death and evil, and therefore can be free to live gratefully and to manifest our gratitude through our care for the neighbor, the people of God, and for the world. It is very freeing to know that the presence of God is practiced by acts of grateful service. It makes all the difference. Prayer and service are what life is about. It is how the Spirit of God reveals God to you. Prayer and service are at the heart of following Jesus.

WE HAVE COME to the end of what I wanted to share with you about following Jesus. May my words be little seeds planted in your heart. Don't worry now what it was all worth, but trust that a seed has been planted. Maybe it is next week or next year that you say, "Something happened by reading that book that is now coming to fruition." Trust it. It may be a new idea. It may not be very specific. You have to believe that God came to you in this book and that one day you will be able to say to yourself, "I never realized it, but something started in me of which I now can see the fruits." You may not know it yet, but you can trust, it will be revealed to you one day. God has given you the promise.

Dear Lord,

Speak gently in my silence.
When the loud outer noises of my
surroundings and the loud inner noises of my

fears keep pulling me away from you, help me to trust that you are still there even when I am unable to hear you. Give me ears to listen to your small, soft voice saying: "Come to me, you who are overburdened, and I will give you rest . . . for I am gentle and humble of heart." Let that loving voice be my guide.

AMEN

(*from* With Open Hands)

EDITOR'S NOTE

This book is based on six talks by Henri Nouwen delivered over Lent at St. Paul Church in Cambridge, Massachusetts, in 1985. It was an uncertain time in Nouwen's life. Two years earlier, after a long and painful discernment, he had returned from a missionary effort in Peru. Feelings of isolation and restlessness followed him from South America to Harvard Divinity School, where he took a prestigious teaching position. But the competitive and ambitious atmosphere of the university only added to his already pervasive feelings of loneliness and unease. These talks—about how to live in anxious times—are so vibrant with energy because the topic was not theoretical to Henri Nouwen; it was his reality. The question of how to follow Jesus was *his* question. Less than four months later, he would leave his tenured position at Harvard, move to Toronto, and become the pastor for L'Arche Daybreak, one of a network of communities founded by Jean Vanier for and with people with intellectual disabilities. By articulating his vision for what it meant to be a follower of Jesus for these talks, Nouwen clarified his own vocational path.

The original content of Nouwen's talks was pre-served on audiotapes of poor sound quality, from which I made transcriptions. Two other sources were used to ensure accuracy: handwritten, point-form notes that Nouwen prepared for himself in advance of the Harvard meditations, and tapes of a talk, on the same theme, that Nouwen gave in Cork, Ireland, the following year. All of this source material is from the Henri J. M. Nouwen Archives and Research Collection at the University of St. Michael's College, University of Toronto.

When I listened to the tapes for the first time, I felt Nouwen speak to me directly, intent that I grasp what he had discovered and desiring passionately that I "get" it. I wanted to preserve this feeling and have tried to capture, as much as possible, the experience you or I would have had attending one of his talks.

Try to reserve judgment on whether you agree or disagree with this or that point in these talks; ask in-stead whether the issues Nouwen brings up connect with your own experience. If so, how? Nouwen does not strive to be right or win an argument. Rather, he seeks to be a channel for your own self-discovery.

My hope is that Nouwen's words take root in your innermost being and that you get what you need in order to find your way home.

Gabrielle Earnshaw, Editor

April 29, 2019

Toronto, Canada

ACKNOWLEDGMENTS

Transcribing and editing these talks by Henri Nouwen was a privilege. The long hours spent listening was like a meditation. I am grateful to Karen Pascal and other members of the Henri Nouwen Legacy Trust for entrusting me with this important and life-giving work.

Yet, for all the time I was working alone, it was not a solitary project. Many people helped to bring this book to life.

I first want to mention Jutta Ayer, a friend and former student of Henri's who attended the original talks in 1985. Jutta, with her singular kindness, provided me with personal and practical assistance, for which I am very grateful.

Another central person in this project was Peter Weiskel, Henri's former administrative assistant, editor, and friend, who was working with Henri at the time of the talks. Peter read my draft manuscript and made salient changes and suggestions. He affirmed that I had captured Henri's voice while ensuring the book read well. His time and effort are greatly appreciated; his stamp of approval is priceless.

The team at Convergent was wonderful to work with. My editor, Gary Jansen, trusted my judgment and gave me the space I needed, yet stepped in at the right moments with flashes of brilliance that greatly improved the book. Other members of the Penguin Random House team, including Ashley Hong, Cathy Hennessy, Mark Birkey, Songhee Kim, Jessica Sayward Bright, and Sarah Horgan, helped to create the beautiful book you are now holding.

Sally Keefe Cohen and Judith Leckie, along with Karen Pascal, fellow members of the Publishing Committee for the Henri Nouwen Legacy Trust, were enthusiastic cheerleaders as well as discerning readers. Sally took care of permissions with her lighthearted but laser-sharp efficiency, and Judith did a careful reading of the first draft and thereafter, and offered sustained support and encouragement. Karen provided excellent guiding suggestions, unbridled trust, and important practical support. Thank you all.

Ray Glennon, a Nouwen Board member and friend, read through the first draft and gave me useful feedback.

Liesl Joson and Simon Rogers, at the Henri J. M. Nouwen Archives and Research Collection, were proficient and helpful with the research questions I threw their way. Thank you both.

Gary Vaughn, of Up Is Loud Productions, provided

vital help improving the sound of the audiotape recordings. This book literally would not have happened without his expertise and skill.

Carolyn Whitney-Brown, Henri's friend and now mine, provided support and encouragement with her characteristic wit and sagacity.

Catherine Smith, Catherine Manning, Roy Schaeffer, Lindsey Yeskoo, Bridget Ring, and Brad Ratzlaff have been my boosters and my friends. Betsy Anderson, Ann Rowland, Lyn Gaetz, Lynne Brennan, John Olthius, and Paula Nieuwstraten from my church community receive my gratitude for their unwavering support of this project. Individually and collectively, these friends have made all the difference.

Special thanks to Laurent Nouwen, Henri's brother, for promoting this book in Holland and Germany and for all he does to further Henri's legacy in his home country. Laurent has shared his love and affection for his brother generously. Much of what I know of Henri's essence is because of him.

As ever, Sue Mosteller, Henri's close personal friend and literary executrix, was unfailing in her enthusiastic support of this project. Her belief in me is the wind in my sails.

I wish to express my gratitude to Richard Rohr for his generous introduction that identifies Henri Nouwen as one of those spiritual teachers who will stand the test of time. This endorsement from a wisdom teacher for our generation is a gift to Henri's legacy. Special mention goes to Jenna Bourland, Richard's assistant, for helping with logistics.

My family deserves final thanks, including my sisters, Heidi Earnshaw and Christine Earnshaw-Osler, and my mother, Marlene Gordon. Don Willms, my husband, who has been listening to me talk about Henri Nouwen for nearly twenty years now, deserves the final bow of gratitude. He listens, reads, edits, critiques, and asks provoking questions. He traveled alongside me through the seasons of the editing process and never tired. Much love and appreciation to you, Don.

Also available from Henri Nouwen

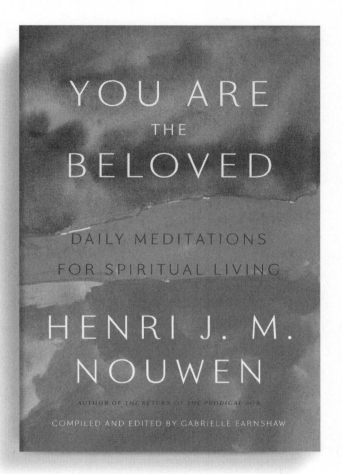

YOU ARE
THE
BELOVED

DAILY MEDITATIONS
FOR SPIRITUAL LIVING

HENRI J. M.
NOUWEN

AUTHOR OF *THE RETURN OF THE PRODIGAL SON*

COMPILED AND EDITED BY GABRIELLE EARNSHAW

"These graceful selections from Nouwen's writings
contain hopeful thoughts for every day of the year."
—*Publishers Weekly*

 CONVERGENT

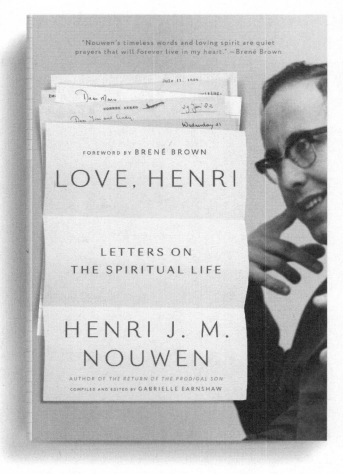

"Nouwen's timeless words and loving spirit are quiet prayers that will forever live in my heart." —Brené Brown

FOREWORD BY BRENÉ BROWN

LOVE, HENRI

LETTERS ON
THE SPIRITUAL LIFE

HENRI J. M.
NOUWEN

AUTHOR OF *THE RETURN OF THE PRODIGAL SON*
COMPILED AND EDITED BY GABRIELLE EARNSHAW

"*Dear Henri,*

Your timeless words and loving spirit are quiet prayers that will forever live in my heart.

Love,
Brené "
　　　—Brené Brown, from the Foreword

CONVERGENT

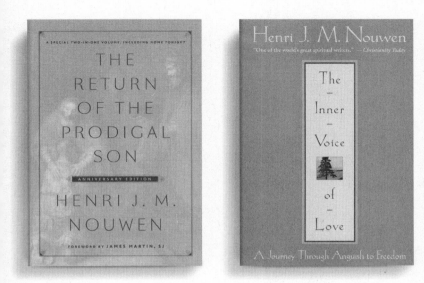

A SPECIAL TWO-IN-ONE VOLUME, INCLUDING HOME TONIGHT

THE
RETURN
OF THE
PRODIGAL
SON

ANNIVERSARY EDITION

HENRI J. M.
NOUWEN

FOREWORD BY JAMES MARTIN, SJ

Henri J. M. Nouwen

"One of the world's great spiritual writers." —Christianity Today

The
—
Inner
—
Voice
of
—
Love

A Journey Through Anguish to Freedom

The
WOUNDED HEALER

Ministry in Contemporary Society

In our own woundedness, we can become a source of life for others

HENRI J. M. NOUWEN

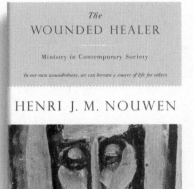

HENRI J. M. NOUWEN
AUTHOR OF THE INNER VOICE OF LOVE

REACHING OUT

THE THREE MOVEMENTS
OF THE SPIRITUAL LIFE

◀ CONVERGENT

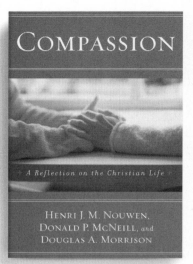

COMPASSION

A Reflection on the Christian Life

HENRI J. M. NOUWEN,
DONALD P. McNEILL, *and*
DOUGLAS A. MORRISON

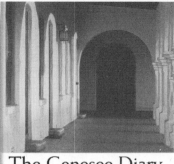

The Genesee Diary

Report from
a Trappist
Monastery

Henri J. M. Nouwen
AUTHOR OF *The Inner Voice of Love*

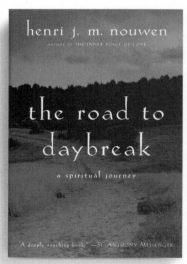

henri j. m. nouwen
AUTHOR OF *THE INNER VOICE OF LOVE*

the road to
daybreak

a spiritual journey

"A deeply touching book" —St. Anthony Messenger

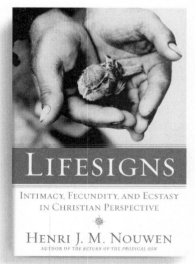

LIFESIGNS

INTIMACY, FECUNDITY, AND ECSTASY
IN CHRISTIAN PERSPECTIVE

HENRI J. M. NOUWEN
AUTHOR OF *THE RETURN OF THE PRODIGAL SON*

CONVERGENT

248.482
NOU

Nouwen, Henri J. M.

Following Jesus.

$23.00

DATE			